Advance praise for The Colonel's Way

Who needs a new kind of hero when you have the original ? And Hollywood ready- *The Colonel's Way!*

Mike Seares; Screenwriter

The Colonel's Way is a tribute to the remarkable life of Colonel Arthur L. Shreve, Jr. who survived against unbelievable odds, never breaking faith with his family, his country or his God. Fully aware that discovery of his documents would mean certain death, Shreve compiled a record of Japan's treatment of the Americans which became indisputable evidence in the ensuing Pacific war crimes trials. *The Colonel's Way* will reignite your sense of patriotism and faith, proving without a doubt that Americans can endure any hardship.

George A. Crawford, Lt. Col., USAF (ret)
Author of Manhunting: Reversing the Polarity of Warfare

The Colonel's Way presents a remarkable portrait of your grandfather. His diaries are a fascinating and moving tribute to the power of the human spirit. He, and the other officers to whom he gives much credit, were the glue that held the men and their mission together. That mission- to survive and to go home.

George F. Obrecht, Attorney;
Secret Service (ret)

THE

COLONEL'S WAY

The legacy you leave is the action you take —

Heather Shea

THE
COLONEL'S WAY

The Secret Diaries of a P.O.W.
COL. ARTHUR LEE SHREVE, Jr.
The Philippines; 1941-1945

Historical Context and Biographies
By Heather P. Shreve

Lt. Arthur Lee Shreve, Jr. ~ October 20, 1923

The Colonel's Way copyright ©2014 by Heather P. Shreve/
The Perrine Company, Inc.
Third Edition with revisions: April, 2015

All rights reserved. No reproduction of this book, in whole or in part, or in any form
may be made without exclusive permission from the copyright owner.
Cover design, illustrations, text © 2014 by Heather P. Shreve
Diaries courtesy of The National Archives ı College Park, MD

Published in the USA.

The Colonel's Way

TABLE OF CONTENTS

Foreword- **13**

Introduction- **17**

The War - **19**

The People - **29**

Diary One – **57**

Diary Two – **109**

Diary Three – **167**

Diary Four - **207**

*Epilogue -***265**

Extra Photographs - **274**

Terms and Abbreviations - **285**

References & Notes- **287**

About The Author – **289**

The Colonel's Way

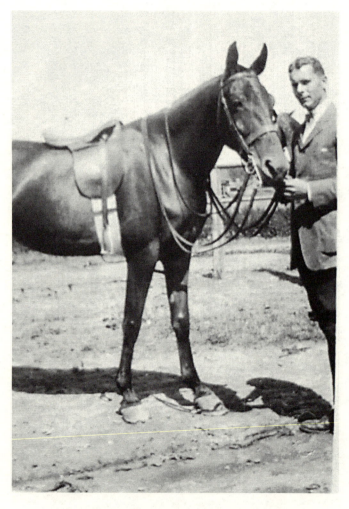

Arthur and one of his horses at Fort Sill, Oklahoma.

IN DEDICATION:

To Arthur... and all men like him.

It can be said
in the best moments of life
when we are touched
by special people
they do not merely leave
behind an impression
but a certain spark;
an incandescence
which will live on in our
hearts and minds
and make us feel the most alive.
They leave us the greatest gift;
the very essence of inspiration,
which will persist long past
the life of family and friends
and even their greatest
accomplishment.
The light of a hero never goes out.

H.P. Shreve

The Colonel's Way

FOREWORD
By Alfred Emile Cornebise

It is difficult to imagine the intensity and persistency of the suffering endured by those incarcerated behind the wire of the prisoner-of-war camps, those "theaters of cruelty and the absurd," maintained by the Japanese during World War II. There is now a book, *The Colonel's Way,* a graphic and compelling account, which focuses on these matters. This cogent presentation, edited by Heather Perrine Shreve, consists of the secret diaries of her grandfather, Colonel Arthur Lee Shreve, Jr., who was a POW–prisoner-of-war–from April, 1942 to the end of the war. He was an artillery officer who fought in the Philippines from the outset of the war until the capitulation of American forces there in April of 1942.

These remembrances are among the most detailed available. They invite readers to probe the parameters of his years-long endurance and perseverance in the face of harrowing situations and the unremitting horror and deep uncertainty endured daily for seemingly endless years. Food was always a problem, and the men often depended on their own vegetable plots, giving a new meaning to the word, "victory garden." Nonetheless, occasionally the Red Cross was able to send in food packages, which, though frequently pilfered by the Japanese, were often the margin of life and death. Medical equipment and supplies were either scarce or nonexistent. There were many instances when razor blades were used as substitutes for scalpels, for example. To be sure, the conditions at each camp were wholly dependent upon the attitudes and views of the camp commanders. Some were harsher than others, and prisoners were spared their lives–or were doomed to die–in these capricious circumstances.

There are other dimensions disclosed in this book that are missing in similar accounts. One was the existence of a shadowy underground network, known as MIS-X. This gathered intelligence regarding general conditions in the Japanese occupied areas, but also enabled prisoners to conduct clandestine negotiations regarding the obtaining of funds from home and to enhance, to the degree possible, additional food and supplies not otherwise obtainable. It was also able to obtain war news, in both Europe and the Pacific, an ongoing avenue of hope. This organization dated from January, 1942, early in the war. It included American army personnel, Philippine Army officers, and heroic Filipino civilians. It operated in the POW camps as well, with Shreve, among others, closely involved. Managing to infiltrate the Japanese system, the organization rendered great service during the war years for many Allied agencies. The apparatus was disbanded after the Americans were once more in command in the Philippines on March 15, 1945.

Among the most dramatic of the diaries' contents concern the transporting of prisoners from the Philippines to Japan. In October of 1944, Shreve was moved from the prison camp at Cabanatuan where he had first arrived in 1942. He was transferred to Bilibid Prison near Manila. There the prisoners endured, as did the Japanese conquerors, numerous American air raids that accompanied the American re-conquest of the Islands. In view of these developments, Shreve, and many other American POWs, were slated to be sent to Japan. Shreve's first transport, however, which he boarded on December 13, was sunk two days later in Subic Bay, during an air raid, the American airmen not knowing that the ship was occupied by American POWs. The loss of lives was considerable, though Shreve was able, not only to swim to shore, but to rescue many of the prisoners who were disabled or unable to swim.

Shreve then boarded another transport that sailed from the Philippines to Takao on Formosa. There, he transferred to another ship bound for Japan. This was also sunk during an air raid while at dock on January 11, with the loss of many additional American POWs. Finally, Shreve, on yet another vessel, arrived in Japan on January 30. On this ship, as on all the others, the conditions were horrific beyond imagination, and many prisoners lost their lives by suffocation in the befouled, almost airless, claustrophobic holds with little water and food. In Japan, Shreve once more had to exert his by now well-honed survival skills to persevere for yet additional months of captivity. Often on the edge, he survived, though he weighed a mere 96 pounds at the time of his rescue in late September, 1945. He was speedily on his way to the United States. Remarkably, throughout, he heroically maintained his basic integrity and humanity and gave unstintingly of himself to help many of his fellow captives.

Though Shreve was able to send infrequent cards and letters home, missives from his family were often delayed for months by the Japanese in yet another form of calculated punishment. His receipt of these letters remained one of the few glimmers of hope during his years in captivity and no doubt played a major role in maintaining sanity.

Those who were safe at home also experienced sufferings of other sorts, no less harrowing, if of different kinds, magnitudes and poignancy. Shreve's wife did not learn of his being in captivity for a year after his incarceration. Previously, she had been informed that he was MIA–missing in action. Meanwhile, she endured her own dislocations, trials and tribulations. In any case, after what must have seemed an eternity, the much-delayed reunion with her husband occurred.

As a vivid testimonial regarding what human beings are capable of enduring under interminable stress, this volume is a significant addition to the literature of World War II, and recommended to general readers as well as scholars of the period.

Alfred Emile Cornebise
Greeley, Colorado
March 14, 2015

INTRODUCTION
by Heather P. Shreve

I remember him well. As I sat on his knee, we played this game he called; 'blackbirds on a fence.' He would put pieces of black electrical tape on all his fingers and suddenly a piece of tape would disappear and a 'bird' would fly away! As a four year-old I missed the sleight of hand and was always delighted. Now I realize that this was 'classic Arthur;' creating small joys from nothing. That was my last memory of him and I can't tell you how much I wish he'd lived longer than 1969.

The transcriptions of my grandfather's diaries from the War Department in 1945 have been in my files for over ten years. They just sat there, waiting; waiting for *someone* to bring them to the world. I picked them up when I was in my early forties but I wasn't ready to read them yet. However, in 2013, after I wrote the book and the screenplay about my own imprisonment story; [*Caught On the Equator*] and had some serious set-backs of my own, I was ready for his ultimate triumph story. In February 2014, I began research for his screenplay; *The Colonel*, and finished it in September that same year. Then I knew. I knew the world needed to hear his story; his bravery and his uncanny strength of mind and heart **had to be told!**

Through his diaries, which I have the privilege of sharing with you in this book, I have learned of an amazing man who lived an unbelievable life. He had a natural knack for what we now call

'The Four-Way Test;' incredible fairness and an ability to see the whole picture. But it's his consistent compassionate leadership and focus on others which will, at times, overwhelm you. Not just his empathy and caring but his selflessness of putting himself out there every day at the risk of death! I can tell you that he continually "under -sells" himself in these diaries and consistently over –delivers, as you will see by his list of awards. He may have been born at the end of The Gilded Age, but his heart contained enough gold for another generation. And the rest of him? Steel, dipped in stardust.

You can't help but fall in love with a man who is charming, handsome and so devoted to his wife, even with all her flaws, and who always finds the best to love in her. You can't help but respect his undying will to keep his men alive and give them comfort where there was none. A true patriot, whose pragmatic and grateful approach to life, as you will see, kept him alive and countless others under unbearable circumstances.

In this book I will give you just the facts; The War, The People and The Diaries. In future books and through film, I hope to share the whole story of his remarkable life because, even with its perceived tragedies, it was truly a life well-lived by a man who was 'one in a million.' I hope you enjoy the pages to follow. It's history that's never been told, diaries that have never been seen. My grandfather, the Colonel, Arthur Lee- however you refer to him- gives us the best of what humanity has to offer and an approach to life that will never leave you with regrets. You will, I hope, see yourself in him. Or, perhaps someone you know. Thanks to his beautifully written words, he's left the world a stellar legacy in a form that only he could do it~ *The Colonel's Way!*

Heather

THE WAR

{The Philippines}

The Colonel's Way

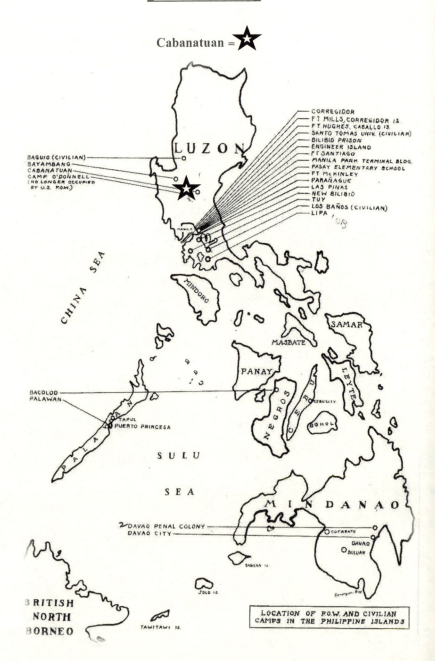

The Colonel's Way

As in life, history proves that catastrophic events are always a series of missteps; a chain of sometimes imperceptible ideas, which come together to create the perfect storm. What happened in the beautiful archipelago of the Philippine Islands in World War II was no different.

At the beginning of the War the Philippines was home to 19 million people and was conveniently and strategically located between Japan and the South Pacific. At this time, these islands were a United States territory, as per the 1898 Treaty of Paris, and so no one was surprised when President Roosevelt called retired Army general, Douglas MacArthur, back into service there in 1941. He was already serving as a Field Marshal in the Filipino military. He was ready and poised to take Roosevelt's $10 M and 100 B-17 Flying Fortress bombers in preparation to mobilize Philippine defenses in case of a Japanese attack. MacArthur deployed most of these defenses on the northern island of Luzon and southern island of Mindanao, forming what he called "key or base point of the U.S. defense line."

Secretary of War, Henry Stimson, and Army Chief of Staff, George Marshall in Washington D.C., believed that their strong presence of American air power in the Philippine Islands would discourage Japanese aggression, but somehow they overlooked the fact that "the greatest concentration of heavy bomber strength anywhere in the world" was lacking the range necessary for a round trip between Clark Field in Philippine Islands and Tokyo. Marshall indicated air fields at Vladivostok would be shared by the friendly Soviet government. He grossly overestimated the Soviet Union's friendliness.

As a precaution, orders were given to move the 27th Bombardment Group B-17 bombers south to Mindanao, out of range of the Japanese bombers. This move was delayed as the pilots were invited to a big party held in the honor of Major

General Lewis Bereton at the hotel in Manila, which also was MacArthur's residence. This event was held during what was to become the night before the Japanese attack.

When the party ended at 0200 hours Manila time, it was 0800 hours in Pearl Harbor when the first Japanese aircraft dropped their torpedoes. As it was too dark to coordinate an offensive operation against the Japanese, the Americans and the Filipinos did what they could in a few precious hours to prepare preemptive air strikes and strengthen ground defenses. Furthermore, at dawn, an unexpected heavy fog over Taiwan would further hamper Japanese air operations. This opportunity was forfeited. Meanwhile, Bereton did his best in getting his aircraft in the air and then waited for MacArthur's approval to attack the invasion fleet or the Japanese bases on Taiwan, however MacArthur never gave the order.

By 1100 hours, American aircraft began to land to refuel, and it was not until then, at about 1120 hours, that MacArthur gave his approval, but then it was too late. At 1235 hours, Japanese Army fighters reached the airfield at Iba on the western coast of Luzon, destroying a fleet of P-40 fighters in the process of landing. A short time later, the Del Carmen airfield to the southeast was also attacked, with its outdated P-35A fighters formed little resistance against the more modern Japanese fighters. These attacks would repeat themselves, within days destroying MacArthur's air force. On December 10, with air superiority achieved, General Masaharu Homma ordered the invasion to set forth starting on the 20th. The Japanese Army landed on Mindanao and then Luzon, quickly capturing airfields and other key strategic positions.

Meanwhile, the question of military intelligence was being raised and in January of 1942 Colonel Charles A. Willoughby called a meeting on the island of Corregidor ['The

Rock'] and a new organization was formed called the MIS-X, [the Military Intelligence Service]. It would proceed under the direction of Col. Willoughby [G-2] and USAFFE, [United States Armed Forces Far East], under the command of Brigadier General Simeon de Jesus in Bataan. De Jesus would start from scratch in his induction of personnel. It would be made up of mostly officers in the Philippine Army and loyal Filipino civilians. One of those civilians was Mr. Fred Threatt [American] who is mentioned in the diaries. He is the driver who brings the Japanese supply truck back and forth from Manila and Cabanatuan City with food and supplies to Camp Cabanatuan.

Before Bataan falls, de Jesus tells Lt. Maceda, one of his operatives, to escape to Manila so the MIS-X can continue from there. Lt. Maceda, a supply officer, arrives on April 12th and after learning the whereabouts of other escaped operatives, sets up a preliminary operation. When de Jesus joins him in Manila in August of 1942, they begin phase II of the covert service. Four American officers were selected in Cabanatuan to be the POC [Points of Contact] for the MIS-X; Col. E. Carl Engelhart, CAC; Lt. Col. Saint,[Corps of Engineers]; Lt. Col. Watrous, Med. Corps, and Maj. Howard Cavender. It would be Carl Engelhart, though, that would receive the first official letter to see if the system would work.

Arthur is aware of all of this, in fact, he signs up for the only detail that would have access with the outside world; the wood cutting detail. This detail consisted of approximately 100 men who were taken to the Sierra Madres Mountains east of camp to cut wood for the kitchens in camp every day. Out there, they have contact with carametta drivers [bull cart drivers] who carry produce to sell but who would prove to be a reliable way to get things back and forth from Cabanatuan City and Manila under the Japanese noses.

The Colonel's Way

From July 1941 to June 1942 the Postal Telegraph Service, the Philippines Civil Service, the Postmasters, the Philippine Long Distance Telephone Co., etc., not only had all been drawn into the interlocking network, primarily for air raid warning and spotting, but also represented a collateral framework of information, transmission, rendezvous and intelligence contacts. Many American businessmen, [miners and plantation owners] were secretly enrolled with a view to forming a nucleus of information and a potential underground in case the Japanese were successful in over-running the islands.

During this time, Colonel Joe Stevenot, an American manager who joined MacArthur's headquarters on Corregidor, maintained a telephone line into the main Manila switchboard [via the Yacht Club cable terminal] and received reports on the Japanese in the city from his intrepid chief operator until the middle of February 1942 when he felt that it was too risky to expose this faithful woman to an obvious death penalty.

By December 1942 Col. Joseph K. Evans, on staff of G-2 Philippine Dept. and an able intelligence operator, had been very active in the development of this clandestine service. Colonel Evans, then in Washington, was one of the first to establish radio contact with Major Praeger, [guerrilla commander; Station WYY], in northern Luzon. Station KFS in San Francisco was able to intercept calls from Luzon and Colonel Evans was instrumental in developing and maintaining a secure cryptographic system with Major Praeger.

In the pre-war months several FBI-trained operatives from Hawaii of Japanese ancestry [Nisei], had been imported to keep the Japanese population in the Philippines under discrete surveillance. Later, these men rendered most important services on Bataan in the interrogation of the prisoners of war, in the translation of captured documents and as CIC [Counter

Intelligence Corps] agents. They highlighted the linguistic potential of the American Nisei which began the modest genesis of the later famous institution-ATIS [Allied Translator & Interpreter Section]. To expedite communications, Gen. de Jesus established a radio station in Manila, located in the projection room of a movie theater. The noise in the projection room masked the sounds of the transmitter, and the crowds in the theater made it possible for the movements of agents to this focal point without attracting attention. The radio station was in operation about six weeks prior to General MacArthur's departure [March 11, 1942] and continued operations undetected until sometime after the fall of Bataan.

The MIS-X operated on the 'cell principle', in groups of three, having a district agent in charge of each surveillance area; San Fernando, San Fernando south to include Manila, the southwest end of Luzon, and the south east end of Luzon. Each district agent would have with him the radio operator and, at the most, one other person from Bataan. Under him three agents were selected from different areas of society: a laborer, a government clerk and a small shop keeper, as an example. Each of these, in turn, would employ three other well-known men to him but the district agent was the only one who knew both the position of the transmitter and of the connection with de Jesus. The Government Postal and Telegraph service and certain selected groups of the Philippine Army Signal Corp were ear-marked to go underground as well, with their radio equipment and await orders.

Nisei operators were parceled out and were able to translate captured documents and soon broke the code of the enemy. One of the signal officers, Major L. Brown, inducted into the service in the Philippines, was the long-time manager of McKay Radio in Shanghai. He was soon able to identify the principal enemy air signals, and air- ground communications, and pick up major air raids and movements. This was the opening wedge to the operations of the central bureau in Australia and Brig. General Carter Clark's brilliant service in Washington. Also, a close liaison was always maintained with the Philippine Constabulary as its best secret operatives later appeared in our counterespionage and in the guerrilla movement. The Philippine department [G-2] employed many special intelligence agents, including a narcotic expert from the U.S. Treasury department.

One of the major players in the Resistance, who was able to completely infiltrate Cabanatuan, is Claire Phillips, a.k.a. "High Pockets," as she hid all her valuables in her bra. She was an Oregon divorcee who moved to Manila with a baby, hoping to find work as a dancer in the nightclubs. There, she met and married Sergeant John Phillips, who was eventually captured and imprisoned in Cabanatuan. Claire, unbelievably, tried to live in the jungles surrounding Cabanatuan so she could be close to him. But, July 27, 1942, she received a note from Chaplain Frank Tiffany [code name: Everlasting] explaining that he had passed away from starvation and other ailments.

Infuriated, she vows revenge and goes deep into the Underground in an attempt to save any and all soldiers that she could. Back in Manila, she obtained a false identity as a Filipina of Italian descent; Dorothy Fuentes. In short order, she opens up a nightclub- The Club Tsubaki- where she begins raising money for her endeavors. Her plan is to also obtain information from the high-ranking Japanese officers who visit the club often and get that back to camp as well. She collects money, notes, medicine, etc. from prominent Manila citizens and- every two weeks -gets it all into Cabanatuan!

She relied on other Filipinas like Evangeline Neibert, [code name: Sassy Suzie] who carried all the 'goods' on the train from Manila to Cabanatuan city. From there- Naomi Flores-

another wife who had lost her husband in Cabanatuan, [code name: Looter], had obtained a vegetable peddler license and worked in the Market. There, she hid the notes and money in the bottom of rice sacks bought by the "rice detail" once a week to be taken back into Camp Cabanatuan. Some of these items magically appeared on the beds of the recipients in camp.[1]

I am sure it was Fred Threatt, the truck driver, who made sure it all found its way to the Commissary, run by Colonel Johnny Johnson, and into the hands of officers like Arthur. Claire was able to persist until May 23, 1944. Then, the Japanese military police apprehended her and took her to the infamous prison, Bilibid. She was tortured and interrogated there until she was liberated by American forces.

It is unknown if the Lt. Maceda [who makes an appearance at Cabanatuan in 1944 in front of Arthur as an interpreter for the Japanese], is the same Lt. Maceda involved in the MIS-X. If it is, they did a remarkable job of infiltrating the Japanese system. In 1944, General de Jesus was also eventually found and arrested by the Japanese Military Police, held in Fort Santiago and then beheaded.

The MIS-X would successfully operate, although fragmented after the fall of Bataan, continually until Gen. MacArthur arrived at Leyte on October 20, 1944 and would be phased out by March 15, 1945 as the war was winding down. The critical information which they gathered was transmitted from radio stations in Luzon to GHQ [General Headquarters] in Australia throughout the Japanese occupation of the Philippines. Information such as troop movement, air activity, shipping, and military installations was all important to the war effort in order to thwart the Japanese at every turn.

Needless to say, it was all very risky business and Arthur navigated it beautifully. As you will read, he was cued into the

MIS-X code; "the home fires", and was one of the reasons he was Morale officer [at one point], keeping the soldiers morale high and "burning" until liberation day.

THE PEOPLE

{Their stories}

The Colonel's Way

The Colonel's Way

COL. ARTHUR LEE SHREVE, Jr.
{July 16, 1897- March 12, 1969}
Serial #0- 011176

"You can only make decisions based on the landscape of the moment." ~ A.L.S.

Arthur was born in Baltimore to Harriett Rebecca Gale and Arthur L. Shreve, Sr. as one of four children. Dorsey and Rosalie Shreve, [his two sisters], and Levin Gale "Bill" Shreve was his younger brother by twelve years. They lived at 127 Lanvale St. in the Bolton Hill section of Baltimore City. Arthur, Sr. was born in 1868 but contracted acute pneumonia and died January 3, 1914 at age forty-five. His father's illness and the impending war seems to spur Arthur into action, something he does best, and on a new path which will change his life, and history, forever.

Arthur's early education started in the Roland Park Country School where he plays some football and becomes team captain. He goes onto high school at Baltimore Polytechnic Institute and is on the lacrosse and tennis teams. But, upon his father's early death, he drops out of high school just months before graduation and goes to work, not even seventeen years old. In the summer of 1914, Arthur is employed at the Roland Park Company as a field surveyor and earns $500.00. After that, he gets hired by the Fidelity & Deposit Company of Maryland as their chief clerk until 1917.

On May 17, 1917 Arthur enlists in the Maryland Army National Guard then is transferred to the Field Artillery in Battery "A" in Anniston, Alabama as a non- commissioned officer. But in short order decides he wants to fly and petitions for a transfer to the Aviation Section, Signal Corps. In order to do this, he has to get recommendations from his employers and other 'respected citizens'. Not surprisingly, he does this with ease, receiving many letters of recommendation including a letter from the president of the Fidelity & Deposit Company, Edwin Warfield, who states; *"...he is the grandson of a very dear friend of mine, Oswald Tilghman, who was the Secretary of State when I was Governor of Maryland, so that this young man is descended from Revolutionary 'stock' and he wants to take part in this great conflict. He is, at present, a member of Battery "A", commanded by my son, but is very anxious to earn a promotion to The Flying Corps. He was employed by this Company for several years and did his work with fidelity and great satisfaction to the Company. I consider him especially fitted for the advancement he seeks, and commend him to your most favorable consideration."*

He also has a letter of the same tone from the president of The National Bank of Maryland, Phillips L. Goldsborough, and so he receives his wish. Next, there's a dazzling whirlwind of activity as he heads towards service in WWI. Assigned Battery "D" in the 110th Field Artillery, he enrolls in the School of Military Aeronautics at the University of Illinois, November 28, 1917. He passes the Aeronautics course and gets his wings. From here he becomes part of 12th Cadet Squadron at Camp Dick, Texas in February 1918. Then he's off to Kelly Field in Texas [now

Lackland Air Force Base] March 1918 as part of the Detachment of Flying Cadets. On June 7, 1918 Arthur is honorably discharged [for a day] so he can be promoted to 2nd Lt., Aeronautical Squadron at Kelly Field the next day- June 8, 1918- and takes the Oath of Office. He wouldn't have been a complete flying cadet until he was enrolled in Machine Gun School at Wilbur Wright Field  [now Wright-Patterson AFB] in Ohio on July 21, 1918. Arthur is sent overseas on September 15, 1918 where he takes an advanced flying course at Issoudun, France at the 3rd Aviation Instruction Center [arriving September, 20]. He flies for the Allies as part of the 2nd Aero Squadron during the war, then is honorably discharged February 18, 1919 and returns to Baltimore.

Upon returning, he gets a job as a Field Engineer with the biggest construction company in Maryland [which remains so today]; The Whiting-Turner Construction Co. By 1920, he must have felt that military life was his calling and decides to apply for a regular commission in the United States Army. Again, he needs recommendations to do so, and receives many glowing letters on his behalf. One is from the president of The Whiting- Turner Co., G. W. C. Whiting himself, dated July 15, 1920. It reads in part; "...*his duties requiring him, at times, to handle large numbers of men, which he has done very efficiently. He is a good engineer, capable and skilled in his line. We believe Mr. Shreve would make you a valuable Officer and we are sorry that he is determined to leave us to go to the Army.*"

The Army offers him the rank of 2nd lieutenant again, and he advocates on his behalf for the rank of 1st lieutenant. In a letter to the Adjunct General he writes; *"Taking into consideration my service in the past emergency and the amount of time I spent in the air...I feel it would be doing myself an injustice to accept the commission of the same rank in which I served during the last emergency..."* However, his commission request is denied and he enters the Field Artillery beginning July 1, 1920 as a 2nd lieutenant. Arthur is officially a 'mustang' now; a commissioned officer who began an armed services career as an enlisted soldier.

In 1921, he is off to Honolulu to serve under the Commanding General of the Hawaiian Department, General Charles P. Summerall. He plays polo with The U.S. Army Polo Team while in Hawaii and takes a little spill March 24, 1922; breaking his left scapula. From July, 1922 to November, my grandfather is put in charge of The Army Service Club in Honolulu, and by the end of that year he is promoted to 1st lieutenant. In October of 1922 he receives a letter from General Joseph Kuhn asking him to be his aide-de-camp at Schofield Barracks, which he accepts and where he remains until 1926. In Arthur's efficiency report in 1925 Kuhn says this; *"...an efficient young officer of great promise...of agreeable personality, who has made the most of his opportunities."*

But his stint in Hawaii becomes pivotal in many ways. First, Arthur is exposed to the Japanese culture [yamato damashii] and learns critical elements about "saving face" including the ways of the Samurai soldier- i.e. death before captivity. Secondly, he must have learned the Japanese language, as he able to decipher Japanese characters and even report to the Japanese Commanders in Japanese while a POW. Thirdly, being a student of war strategy, he learns the Japanese Imperial Army's tactics for attack; surprise and terrain before troops. And finally, being on an island, he's exposed to the Coast Artillery and being a 'coast-watcher.' All of this allows him to be a low-profile 'guest' of The Japanese Army, avoiding being flagged and beaten as well as ways to assess the situation and make good "...decisions based on the landscape of the moment."

After Hawaii, on September 16, 1926, he marries Julia 'Judy' McCoy, the love of his life, in Dayton, Ohio where many of her mother's family members [the Barneys] reside. He graduates from the Field Artillery School on June 11, 1927 and then from the Advanced Horsemanship Course in June of 1929. While at Fort Sill, [Oklahoma], their first son is born in 1931; Arthur Lee Shreve III.['Sandy']. In the meantime, Arthur is becoming a crackerjack horseman and is on The U.S. Army Show Jumping Team where he competes with his horses; *Prince Gerald*, '*You'll Do II.*,' and *Valencia*. Around this time, he orders an expensive pair of custom-made boots from Peal & Co. in London. In the only letter I've seen questioning my grandfather, Peal & Co. writes to the Army in 1933

The Colonel's Way

looking for his balance that's still outstanding. [Knowing my grandfather, there was probably a good reason why he hadn't paid them]. While at the Fort Sill Artillery School, he teaches equitation and becomes team captain of both the jumping and polo teams at one point. By 1933 he is promoted to captain and in October, 1935 Arthur is assigned to teach Military Science and War Tactics at the University of Oklahoma as assistant professor. In the meantime, the Great Depression and the Dust Bowl were sweeping across the Mid-west, but the social scene among the military families was going strong. One of Arthur's and Judy's favorite songs was *Smoke Gets in Your Eyes* and another called *Remember Me* ; Bing Crosby, 1937. [There is a line from the latter that becomes significant later]. Their second son is born at Fort Benjamin, Indiana [Douglas McCoy Shreve] in 1936.

By 1938, Arthur's career is winding down and in June of 1939 he is recommended to the Command and General Staff School in Fort Leavenworth, Kansas. In January 1940, [see humorous letter; pg. 37] Arthur was thrown a first-class retirement party by Brig. Gen. William L. Ritchie, [U.S. Air Force], who was a WWII liaison officer between Gen. George C. Marshall,[Army Chief of Staff], and Gen. Douglas MacArthur plus many, many other notable accomplishments.

Arthur is promoted to Major in March of 1940, then Lt. Colonel and retires [or so he thought] to his Maryland farm in Howard County; "Our Decision." [See page 44 for more]. As WWII progressed around the world, Arthur relaxed on his farm for

The Colonel's Way

FORT LEAVENWORTH, KANSAS

December 13, 1939.

Subject: Weak end maneuvers.

To: General A. Shreve

    1. The presence of you and your chief of staff is requested at Field Headquarters of the 1st Army of Salt Creek (Pope Hall Basement), at 7:30 P.M., 20 January, 1940.

    2. You all know what the situation will be at that time.

    3. The newest streamlined terpsichorean maneuvers will be discussed and practiced. (2 additional trucks will be furnished by the Quartermaster to transport the band).

    4. a. Initial and continuous issue of Class I A (liquid) supplies at the railhead at front end of headquarters.

        b. One cooked meal will be issued.

    5. Staff groups will be formed on arrival - draw your assignment - (you may get Hedy Lamar as your G-Whiz).

    6. Usual equipment will be worn (see Post Uniform Regulations).

    7. a. All passive AA measures will be taken - including passouts in case of air raids.

        b. Medical personnel and Red Cross Nurses will be prepared to render 1st aid to air raid casualties.

        c. Security detachments will protect men's overcoats and ladies honor during blackouts.

    8. Required: Your decision.

                                      Wm. L. RITCHIE,
                              Field Marshall (Sounds good anyway).

OFFICIAL:
    ELEANOR P. RITCHIE,
    Chief of Staff.

Note: Decision to be transmitted as soon as practicable by any available means of communication to above C of S at 419-2 Kearney (Phone 7551).

a year until the fateful message came. In June of 1941, he was called back to duty; the Pacific Theatre and the Philippine Islands. Judy and Arthur spent the summer looking for a residence in Baltimore where Judy and the boys could live. They settled on 502 Wingate Road in Roland Park on the edge of Baltimore City. On October 25, 1941 he boards a train from Baltimore bound for San Francisco and then catches a ship to the South Pacific and the Philippine Islands. Arthur reports to Brig. Gen. George Parker, Commander of the South Luzon Force, on November, 21 at Fort McKinley as Chief of Artillery. He and his fellow officers thought they were sent to the best possible place; 'The Pearl of the Orient.'

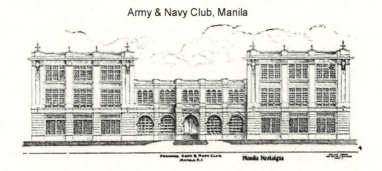

Army & Navy Club, Manila

They dine lavishly at the Army and Navy Club in Manila, a classic white building with beautiful columns and massive arches. They went to the theatre, played polo and rode horses together right up until the eve of Pearl Harbor. Soon, their paradise would turn to unmitigated hell. The diaries take us on a journey from there.

However, several things are never mentioned in his diaries because if they were ever found, the secrets they revealed would have assured Arthur's execution by the Japanese, and others, like Claire Philips. My suspicion is that Arthur knows all about "High Pockets" but never dares to allude to her 'work' in any of his writings. It was already against Army regulations to even keep personal diaries while on 'duty.' We know that Arthur builds a crystal radio receiver in the bottom of his Army canteen, but now, according to *Blood Brothers*, an account by senior medic Dr. Eugene Jacobs, we know more about the *'how.'* After several months of hearing no news, some "clever Americans" decided to build a radio. At night, several American captives operated the generators which ran the electricity and the water pumping station. When they suspected that the Japanese were listening to their radios, the POWs on duty would run up the voltage and blow out their radios. In the morning, the Japanese asked the "clever Americans" to fix the radio².

Arthur is asked by the Japanese C.O. to repair the radio, and he's prepared. He asks for two of everything, and when he receives the replacements, he takes the old parts for himself and builds a receiver in the 'canteen with the false bottom.' He uses it to "listen in" on the Japanese and surrounding radio stations. Soon, they have news and he passes it to people like Fred Threatt, [the American internee who drove the Japanese supply truck] who takes it back to town with him and who is certainly part of the MIS-X. Eventually, the Japanese ask *them* for news!

He also never goes into detail in the diaries about a major Japanese landing in which he was directly involved. In his sworn testimony at the Pentagon in 1953, my grandfather explains more about what he saw when he first arrived in the Philippines- and the strategic landscape- particularly Atimonan Bay. In December of 1941, my grandfather went and surveyed the artillery around Luzon. He reported to General Parker what he saw as a weakness on the east side; their "back door" was open at Atimonan Bay. The Navy thought the bay was too shallow for a large amphibious force, but Arthur knew better. He saw a perfect landing place, hidden by a peninsula,[really an island] that the Japanese could hide behind before making landfall.

In repeated requests to the brass, including General Parker -who sends Arthur directly to General MacArthur two days in a row- his requests for artillery are turned down. Instead, Arthur took it upon himself [with Parker's blessing] to turn at least two of his six guns towards the bay. At 4 AM on December 24, 1941 my grandfather went looking for his main Reconnaissance Officer who was asleep in a little hotel along the shores of Atimonan. As he rousts him from a deep sleep, a Filipino woman declares, "Look!" My grandfather looks out the window, and [as stated in his testimony] he watches as the Japanese Army brings into Atimonan Bay two huge aircraft carriers, a large destroyer and a couple of cruisers, along with forty transport boats who put ashore a large reinforced regimental combat team. They had no choice but to retreat and The Fall of Bataan begins. Arthur is now ordered to go to the 51st Philippine Division to help General Albert M. Jones, now a defense force. Clearly, if they had listened to my grandfather, things would have turned out very differently.

We know Arthur collaborates with officers like Colonel Engelhart, the camp interpreter, and is part of the reason Arthur keeps such meticulous diaries. And, of course, Colonel Johnson and Arthur organize and collaborate the entire time to smuggle in supplies. But what about the carametta drivers who Arthur saw during the day in the Sierra Madres mountains? They are cited in a declassified document from the Army that they were certainly probable "helpers" in the resistance against the Japanese. Could he have run into his old house boy out there? And what about the Japanese M.P.'s who colluded with them [the POWs] to smuggle in goods and supplies? And where were his diaries actually buried? According to sworn testimony in 1953 by my grandfather, there originally were 5 diaries; one he left with an unknown man at the prison hospital, which was passed onto a Private of the 640th Battalion and turned into the Army. The second, he left with a man named Tom Bell, who was with Arthur in the field hospital when he had his attack of appendicitis and who was sent home as he lost a leg. Mr. Bell got as far as San Francisco and was searched and the diary was handed over, we assume to the Army since I have the transcriptions. We do know Arthur wrote the diaries in Filipino composition school books but only the War Department and his brother Bill Shreve know where they were buried around Cabanatuan.

So many questions remain. And, how deep was Arthur in the Underground and the MIS-X? How did he [and those who helped him] cash checks against his bank in Howard County, Maryland? I am sure we will never know from these diaries alone. I can only say, he was always a very clever man with a powerful purpose who left no stone unturned.

JULIA PERRINE McCOY
{ October 8, 1904 – February 15, 1987 }

Julia ['Judy'] was born in Richmond, Virginia to Julia Henrietta Barney and Jay Pollock McCoy who lived on Jamestown Island. Edward Everett Barney, Judy's grandfather, bought Jamestown Island in 1889 along with a great deal of other Virginia land. Judy grew up on the island and crossed the James River on a ferry to ride a horse and buggy to school in Williamsburg. Judy's twin brother, Jay McCoy [by all accounts] was addicted to alcohol and died in 1977. Unfortunately, Judy got the same genetics and was also susceptible to alcohol her whole life; especially during the war years when Arthur was interned.

If it wasn't for a fortuitous visit by ocean liner to Honolulu, Hawaii in the early 1920s with her mother, Judy would have never met Arthur. Somehow, they met by chance... and the love affair began. Judy shared some common life experiences with Arthur, namely that they both lost their father before they were twenty and they both liked to read. My grandmother apparently was quite a character and I am sure kept Arthur on his toes.

During the time Arthur was interned, Judy took up being a 'Gray Lady' and drove an ambulance for the Red Cross. She cared for her growing boys and visited the Plimhimmon Hotel [a hotel that Arthur's grandmother had started] every summer. The remainder of their summers were spent on their farm; Our Decision. At first, Judy knows her husband is alive. She receives his first telegram in November, 1941. But her first letter to him in early December is sent back. By the following June [1942], she gets a letter from the

```
                    IMPERIAL JAPANESE ARMY

1. I am interned at The Philippine Military Prison Camp #1.
2. My health is — excellent; good·fair·poor
3. I am — uninjured; sick in hospital·under treatment·under treatment
4. I am — improving·not improving·better; well.
5. Please see that your health, pictures of boys, planting
   of fruit and other trees and lawn are     taken care of.
6. (Re: Family); Love to our boys and mothers, sisters,
   and brothers.  All mine to you.  I love you.
7. Please give my best regards to  Sloan, Carroll, and all.
```

War Department saying he is 'Missing in Action.' Finally, in December '42, she gets confirmation he is a POW. For Judy, and for all military wives, the uncertainty of it all must have been

The Plimhimmon Hotel, Ocean City MD- 1930s

crushing. She began to drink more and more until [I was told by her sons] she would drink herself into oblivion every night and cry herself to sleep after they were in bed. She does regain contact with Arthur eventually but in the meantime Judy finds herself in affairs, men who prey on her, which only keeps her in an endless pattern of drinking to numb herself. If she had friends closer [I am sure she made friends while she lived on the forts] they might have

been a great comfort. And her mother, living so far away [in those days] in Virginia, probably made it challenging for Judy to visit, or visa- versa. It makes for a tragic set of circumstances which many women faced. But, she never stopped loving him and she pulled it together for her sons and worked tirelessly on 'Our Decision' which is what Arthur saw in her letters. And, for that, he always admired her.

COL. LEVIN GALE SHREVE
{ February 17, 1910 – May 3, 1998 }
Serial #: O-294544

"Everything great was done by one person...before lunch."
~L.G.S.

When Levin Gale was born in Baltimore the doctor delivering him turned to his mother Harriett and said; "You *can't* call him *Levin Gale!* I'm calling him *Bill*..." And from that point forward, he was 'Bill' Shreve. If it wasn't for Bill, many things would have turned out very differently for Arthur, Judy and others. It was Bill who helped find, expedite and actually transcribed my grandfather's diaries for the War Department in San Francisco in 1944-45 while Arthur was still interned. In fact, if it wasn't for my great uncle Bill, I wouldn't have my grandfathers' memorabilia and personal items including his riding trophies, some photos and even his tiger maple 1830s Kentucky long gun.

The best story involving Bill though, comes around 1938 when Arthur is about to retire and they start thinking of moving and buying a farm in Howard County, Maryland. Arthur sends him a telegram asking him to 'keep an eye out' for a good place. One night Arthur and Judy get a telegram at Fort Sill; it says: *'Found a farm, loved it so much, bought it myself.'* Reportedly, Judy is smoking her normal Chesterfield cigarette and suddenly proclaims to Arthur; "*Goddammit* – Arthur, the next farm we find, it's going to be *our decision*." So, when Judy and Arthur find a farm together in 1939 they call it "Our Decision." Bill was educated at the Episcopal High School in Virginia and went on to graduate from Johns Hopkins University. He married a girl named Barbara Harris in the 1930s. Barbara's mother was a Warfield, and her father was Governor Edwin Warfield of Maryland, [1904-1908]. During WWII, Bill served as a General Staff officer [colonel] on the combined Army- Navy staff of Admiral William F. Halsey in the South Pacific and later at Headquarters; U.S. Forces China, with General Albert C. Wedemeyer. Thrown into official contact with General Chiang Kai-shek, he was asked personally by Chiang to create a definitive plan for rural reconstruction in Post-war China. After the war, he was awarded two Bronze Stars, and an Air Award for flying one hundred hours over China; '…in extremely hazardous conditions of combat, weather and terrain during the period from August 1, 1945- Nov. 10, 1945.' He also received several Commendation ribbons as well. Bill then joined the C.I.A. where he served in the Middle East, Far East, Washington, Baltimore and Honolulu in a career that lasted more than twenty years. At age seventy, Bill decided to start writing and ended up authoring

several books including *Tench Tilghman; The Life and Times of Washington's Aide-de- Camp; The Phoenix with Oily Feathers* and *The Tides of Sligo*. L.G. is buried in the Warfield family cemetery in Howard County next to Barbara.

CAPT. ARTHUR LEE SHREVE, III.
{January 10, 1931 – July 19, 1995}
Serial #: 0-999269

My father, Sandy, was born in the beginning of The Dust Bowl and the Great Depression in Norma, Oklahoma and was a self-described 'army brat', moving from fort to fort most of his childhood. When the War broke out Sandy and his younger brother; Douglas McCoy Shreve, were left wondering if they would ever see their father again. From age ten to almost fifteen, my dad became 'the man of the house'. At first, they lived at the aforementioned Wingate Road, but when oil prices went sky-high they were forced to move to the Tuscany Apartments nearby. They attended the local public school, went to the movies at The Hamden Theatre on weekends [36th street] and during the summers they always visited the family hotel, The Plimhimmon; named after the Tilghman estate in Oxford, Maryland. At the Plim, as they called it, there was a long-time employee; a black chef named Robert who worked at the hotel for probably 50 years. His parents were most likely slaves as he was born around 1875. My father would tell me of this tall, regal man as he still worked there during the '40s.

The Colonel's Way

The rest of the summers were spent at Our Decision which was just a summer home at this point, with no running water, just electricity to the kitchen and no telephone. For the boys it was a real escape and they had loads of fun running around just being boys. Sandy tended a 'victory' garden there, hauled water from the 'Big Spring' for the house and chased the thousands of fireflies at night. In fact, one night Doug asked his mother; "Ma, when is Pop comin' home?" Her answer was something like this; "Well, I am not sure...but let's catch some fireflies and put them in jars on the fence posts, just in case..." With mason jars in hand,

Sandy and Doug proceeded to catch hundreds of fireflies and set the jars on the fence posts near the driveway entrance to light the way for their dad- just in case.

During this time, Sandy became an Air Warden, and later, head of the Junior Red Cross in Baltimore. Meanwhile, we can only imagine how it must have been without a father at this critical time and to watch his mother fall into despair. I wish he were here so I could hear it again with new ears.

GEN. HAROLD *"Johnny"* JOHNSON
{February 22, 1912 - September 24, 1983}
Serial # 0-019187

Johnny was born in Bowesmont, North Dakota and was a self- described 'country boy' who was at the bottom of his class at West Point. He slowly made his way to the middle by the time he graduated in 1933. In the spring of 1940, Johnny was assigned to the 57th Infantry, the Philippine Scouts, at Fort McKinley. After Pearl Harbor, Johnny was sent to Bataan as a Regimental Operations Officer and later as commander of the 3rd Battalion. He was twenty-nine and already a Lt. Colonel when he met Arthur.

When Bataan falls, he mirrors Arthur's movements throughout. As Commissary Officer at Cabanatuan, he and Arthur begin the process of securing supplies and food for the POWs, which Johnny did with great finesse. When Johnny weighed 90 lbs. at the end in Camp Fukuoka, Japan, an army surgeon who examined him said; "There was no medical reason why Harold Johnson should be alive…" He is fondly remembered in the Armed Forces Journal as such; "…but we venture the opinion that the Army has never had, and perhaps never will, have a greater leader."

COL. DAVID S. BABCOCK
{September 28, 1899 – January 23, 1945}

David, [or 'Bab' as he was later called], was born on Staten Island, New York and was named after his grandfather, Captain David S. Babcock, who commanded two of the most famous clipper ships in New England in the 19th century; *The Young America* and *The Swordfish*. David was also a 'ring-knocker' from West Point [class of 1923], and went on to be assigned to the Field Artillery. Bab must have met Arthur before the war because they were already friends of many years by the time they reached the Philippines. David's first post was Fort Sam Houston, Texas then the Schofield Barracks in Honolulu in 1929. But I suspect they met at Fort Sill, Oklahoma or Fort Benjamin, Indiana. Bab probably bonded with Arthur as he was also a student of riding and polo and was very interested in war tactics, politics and world events. He was a newly-wed when the war broke; married to Roberta Miner.

His specialty was 75 mm guns mounted on half-tracks and he was made Battalion Commander of the experimental Tank Destroyer group in 1941. In Bataan, he was the Commanding Officer of the S. Luzon Provisional Group, F.A. His journey also followed

Arthur's exactly as they were moved from O'Donnell, to Cabanatuan and to Bilibid Prison, and later- the 'hell ships'. While interned, Col. Babcock ran the camp library at Cabanatuan and managed to secretly insert anti- Nazi works and Churchill's speeches into the books that were approved by the Japanese like *Alice in Wonderland* and Filipino school books.

My grandfather was quoted as saying this about David; "Bab served with distinction during the difficult withdrawal from S. Luzon and his battalion was an excellent one which he had gotten together on extremely short notice…serving in it were American soldiers, Philippine Scouts, Philippine Army draftees and even some patriotic Philippine civilians who drove Bab's vehicles. It was a great tribute to his leadership that he could hold so heterogeneous an organization together during the stress of battle." One of the officers in his battalion wrote; "There is no use of me telling you what a wonderful man he was and how much he meant to those of us who had the honor to serve under him."

COL. CARL ENGELHART
{ June 16, 1900 - June 14, 1995}
Serial #: O- 012773

Carl graduated from West Point in 1920 and went on to be one of the most pivotal characters in this story of the Philippines during the Japanese occupation. Carl was in the 91st Div. [The Mine Group] of the famous

The Colonel's Way

Philippine Scouts. But that wasn't his greatest contribution, nor was it that he learned to speak fluent Japanese and was the interpreter in Camp Cabanatuan and everywhere he was needed [although that was very important]. His most interesting contribution to history, though little known, was that Col. Engelhart was picked to be the P.O.C. [Point of Contact] for the MIS-X now operating in Manila. See this declassified letter, [from Intelligence Activities in the Philippines during the Japanese Occupation] below:

SUBJECT: Military Intelligence

TO: Lt. Col: E. Carl Engelhart, C.C. and Lt. Col. Saint, C2, POW Camp, Cabanatuan.

It is directed that you establish an intelligence system within the POW camp to procure and evaluate information on:

a. Enemy activities throughout Luzon, to include:
    1) Corregidor
    2) Bataan
    3) Clark Field
    4) Nichols Field
    5) Ft. McKinley
    6) Manila
    7) Nielson airport

b. Conditions among civilians in populated areas to include:
    1) Status of food and other supplies available to civilians.
    2) Their attitude towards the enemy.

The Colonel's Way

   3) Degree of cooperation to be expected when US. Forces arrive.

c. Conditions existing in the POW camp to include:
   1) Violations of Geneva Convention rules.
   2) Roster of prisoners, alive and dead.
   3) Physical condition of POW.

d. The Jap administrative and guard unit to include:
   1) Number, state of training, unit and officers.
   2) Attitude towards POW, with trend, if any.
   3) Attitude towards the war.

                    C.A. Willoughby
                    Brig. General, U.S. Army,
                    A.C. of S.,G-2.

Throughout the ordeal, Carl interpreted all of the Japanese requests, threats, etc., including the warning from the Japanese commanders on one of the 'hell ships'; the Oryoku Maru: "If anyone other than an officer in charge so much as touches the hatch ladder, he will be instantly shot." Throughout, Colonel Engelhart, and many others, did what was needed with as much dignity and integrity as they could muster to just get out alive.

MAJOR JOE GANAHL
{ April 19, 1903- February 11, 1945 }

Joe Ganahl was born in Louisville, Kentucky and entered West Point in 1923. After a brief but spectacular career in the Air Corps as a student pilot, Joe was transferred to the 12th Field Artillery, at Fort Sam Houston. Next, he served in Hawaii; 13th Field Artillery and 11th Field Artillery Brigade. While in Hawaii he also met his future wife and married her. He became a member of the Battery Officers' class at the Field Artillery School and *ordered* to take the Advanced Course in Horsemanship the next year as his polo skills were exemplary. He was then assigned to the crack 16th Field Artillery battalion at Fort Myer. In 1937, he became an instructor of the 37th Div.; Ohio National Guard while stationed in Cleveland. He joined the Armored Force as Commander of Battery B, 68th Field Artillery, and then was appointed Assistant G-4, 1st Armored Division and joined Arthur in Manila.

In the Philippines, Joe was in command of the 1st Provisional Artillery Battalion [self-propelled guns]. It was a battalion of heterogeneous American soldiers, Philippine Scouts, Philippine Army draftees, and Filipino civilian truck drivers. Within a matter of days, he had organized this group into what the Corps Artillery Commander considered "a marvel of excellence and discipline". Under Joe's command, it was awarded three Distinguished Unit Citations.

Joe was wounded in the head and in the left arm in the Fall of Bataan, however that didn't stop him on the Bataan Death March from carrying an exhausted Catholic chaplain's mass kit; the altar stone and chalice, 80 miles to Camp O'Donnell. Joe also mirrored Arthur's movements through the prison camps and onto the 'hell ships.' Later, General Wainwright would write, "The senior American officers with the 13th and the 12th Infantry regiments; Lieutenant Colonels Moses and Noble, and Major Joe Ganahl, were three of the finest combat officers in my command." Joe would be awarded the Distinguished Service Cross, the Silver Star, the Legion of Merit, and the Purple Heart with three clusters.

MAJOR MARSHALL H. HURT, Jr.
{June 26, 1908- April 3, 1945}

Marshall Hurt was born in Tuskegee, Alabama, the eldest son of Marshall Hurt, Sr. and Josie Lee Hurt. From the start, he had a certain way about him; a sense of purpose and the steadfastness to achieve any goal. He graduated West Point in 1930 and went forward loving every aspect of military life. Like Arthur, he spent three years in Hawaii serving as aide to a general, [although many years after Arthur's stay], in Marshall's case; General Nuttman.

After Hawaii he went back to West Point to teach drawing for four years. In 1940, Marshall was called to the Philippines and was Battalion Commander of the 31st Infantry. This is where my grandfather would have been reunited with him, or met him, as they were both on General King's staff at one point. In the Fall of Bataan, he and another volunteer went forth through dangerous enemy territory to deliver surrender documents to the Japanese field forces. According to Arthur's diary, he also was the guy who, along with Colonel Williams, carried the surrender flag forward the day Bataan fell.

Because Marshall was part of General King's staff, he was afforded the privilege of being driven on The Death March as Arthur was; a small gift from the Japanese. Their movements mirrored each other to some extent; especially in the last year in the ordeal of the three 'hell-ships', Bilibid and Camp Fukuoka. He swam ashore twice, like Arthur, but eventually succumbed to a tropical disease in Camp Fukuoka and passed away suddenly. In my grandfather's diaries, he mentions his death as happening in March, not the reported April. The Colonel also says, he gathered up Marshall's last belongings and was going to attempt to get them back to his loved ones.

My grandfather often speaks of Marshall, always in glowing terms. He was awarded the Bronze Star, and later, the Silver Star posthumously in 1946. He will be remembered as a cheerful and optimistic soldier, according to all reports, not to mention- brave.

The Colonel's Way

The Colonel's Way

DIARY ONE

{November 28, 1941 - September 22, 1943}

The Colonel's Way

The Colonel's Way

DIARY OF ARTHUR LEE SHREVE, Jr.
LT. COL. (F.A.) G.S.C.

My darling Judy,

I have decided to write this, so that in case I do not return to you, that you and our boys will have a record of my comings and goings in the Philippine campaign. May God in his great Mercy allow me to tell you all of myself. For obvious reasons I am refraining from remarks of an intimate nature insofar as I can, as this will in the event of my death pass through many hands before it reaches you; and I care too much to have my feelings aired to prying eyes. This is reconstructed from notes and memory beginning on November 28, 1941 and will continue, God willing, until we are united again. God bless you, my darling, no man could have been blessed as I have been in you. I love you.

/s/
Arthur

November 29, 1941

At last my orders have been put through, and although I have yet to receive them, I left Manila this morning and reported to Brigadier General George Parker, C.G. of the south Luzon Force. This force corresponding to a corps is composed of two Philippine divisions: one commanded by Col. Jones, Inf., U.S.A.; one by Brigadier General Lim, [Philippine Army], and two regular of Philippine Constabulary. I am assigned to Force Quartermaster. General Parker was having a conference with his division and other commanders; order from USAFFE to reconnoiter beach positions for immediate occupation when ordered. General Parker was very pleasant, making me feel quite a home.

November 30

I spent the day getting settled in at headquarters. Unpacked my things. I am very comfortable with a chair, table and magazine rack I got from the Post Exchange. I have a house boy to clean and wash for me.

December 1

Spent the day at the 41st with General Lim and the 51st, [Colonel Jones], divisions in an effort to find the status of supply and to get the records of the division in Q.M. in order. Things are in fair shape. There is a shortage of all types of supplies and equipment.

December 2

General Parker today offered me the post of Chief of Artillery of the Force. This has the approval of the USAFFE, of course I accepted with pleasure. I am to act in both capacities temporarily.

December 3rd, 4th and 5th

Have spent these days familiarizing myself with the artillery of S. Luzon Force. At present, there is Corps Artillery: W. W. Scott [Maj., F. A.] commanding. Consists of 3 two gun batteries, G.P.F.s, model 1917. Organized as first battalion, 86th Field Artillery, [P. S.] The batteries were emplaced when I took over as follows: 1 battery covering Batangas Bay, 1 battery covering Balayan Bay, 1 battery at Nassugbu (Town) covering the harbor there. I was not satisfied with the position at Nassugbu or Batangas. Have ordered both changed- one gun a time. The 41st division has its artillery, short of fire control, equipment and trucks. Its armament consists of two batteries of 2.95 Howitzers and 4 batteries of British 75 mm guns with wooden wheels. 51st division artillery is in the process of being mobilized in south Luzon. It is due to begin its assembly in the training area Saturday, December 6th. At present, it has no armament.

December 6

I spent the morning in the cantonment and training area awaiting the arrival of units of the 51st division. Trains were late. The one due to arrive at 6:00 AM arrived at 10:00 AM. I could not wait for the one due at 8:00 AM. The trains contain the remainder of the 51st Division [infantry] and part of the Field Artillery. After reporting to headquarters, I spent the remainder of the afternoon stowing my gear. Major Bennett, who is to be Force G – 4, moved in with me. I believe the high regard O.O. Wilson holds for him is justified. We went to the A & N club for dinner. Sat around the bar after dinner.

December 7

Horseback riding with Captain Neiger, A. D. C. Then to Manila with Bennett for late lunch at the A & N club. Then to see "*Hold Back the Dawn.*" Very good. Back to the club for late supper and home. Early to bed.

December 8

It is well that Bennett and I came home early, as at 4:00 AM Wilson [G-1] called me to give me the news that Pearl Harbor had been bombed and that we were in an undeclared war. A conference was called by General Parker at 5:00 AM. MacDonald; Inf.

Commander of Staff, Wilson G-1, Moore G-2, Johnson G-3, Bennett G-4, Neiger A.D.C., and myself, Commander of Artillery and acting Q. M., were there. No details as to the result of the attack were known. Troops ordered to beach positions. All of us on 24- hour duty. I awakened Scott, C. O. of the heavy artillery, and gave him the news. He left for his Command post at Batangas. Routine work at headquarters and packing up my things, moving to the Command post which is at Fort McKinley, occupied the rest of the day. Baguio, Clark field, and our fields at Aparri and Iba were all bombed. We lost a lot of planes.

December 9

Early this AM, awakened by the sound of planes. They passed northwest of us and bombed Nichols Field and the Pan American radio station. The result was too accurate for night bombing. We suspect 5th column. I spent the rest of the day checking the training and equipment of the Divisional Artillery of the Force. The 41st is fair. The 51st is in bad shape, not to complete its mobilization until December 15th and yet to arrive in the training area. Equipment is short and it being the last, it will suffer. Searight is in command, an excellent officer.

December 10

I made a swing through part of our sector visiting the command post of the 51st and 41st divisions. While at the 41st {Tagaytay} a large formation of H- bombers came over. But they went north in the direction of Manila Bay. I learned later that they bombed the naval base at Cavite with devastating results. Heavy casualties in ships and men suffered by us. Back late at night, after bad ride with a Filipino driver not used to driving without lights in the rain and fog.

December 11

Much air activity over Nichols field which is close to Fort William McKinley, bombing and strafing. I've packed the last of my things. When I will see them again, who knows. My best woolens I've stored in cold storage in Manila. I saw one of our B-17's attacked by three Jap zero fighters. Our bomber was headed south. He drove off two of the zeros and as they went out of sight the B-17 pulled away from the last attacker. We have had to hit the ditch a lot these days.

December 12

After so much activity during the days and night bombing of Nichols some of the more cautious members of the staff, including me, decided to sleep in the tunnel which is about completed here. One night is enough. I will take my chances in the open from now on. I felt a little foolish when I came into the Command Post this AM. I have no one to help me except a lieutenant which is liaison officer from the 86th field artillery. General Parker assures me that we will soon get some personnel for our headquarters. I will get my share. First, some part of the artillery. Each day, the 41st has had no target practice. After much difficulty, I get authority for them to shoot. Much fear of the effect of fire on the Filipinos.

December 13

Busy with efforts to get equipment for the field artillery. South Luzon is to get one battalion of the self- propelled mounts. Colonel David S. Babcock commanding.

December 14

The Japanese landed in the south end of our sector, 8 to 10 transports and one aircraft carrier. We have ordered some English troops and one battalion of infantry, all P. A., to intercept them. The landing was made at Legazpi at the south tip of Luzon. We are to move our command post to Binan. The bombings and strafings continue at Nichols Field, Clark and the field at Batangas. I passed Nichols Field today. The remaining ships are well disbursed in the available cover. A.A. batteries nearby look efficient.

December 15

We moved by echelon yesterday but we are now established in what was a native dance hall and bodie house. We are blacked out at night and allow no cars or trucked to stop within 500 yards. I have been assigned a car with the driver and have a tiny office for the artillery headquarters; still no personnel. I used the liaison detail from the 86th F.A. The remainder of the 51st battalion artillery is on route to the divisional area. I will be glad to see Pat Searight again. The Japanese landed on Vigan on the 14th, small force.

December 19

Full day. I am out in the field or down to see General King, the USAFFE Chief of Artillery. E. G. Williams, now full colonel, is his Executive officer. So I have a nice reception every time I go there. The remainder of the 51st field artillery has arrived in the division area. Only one of the three battalions have been equipped with guns, the British 75 mm. with wooden wheels. There are not enough sites to equip all guns. Telephones and other signal and optical equipment are short. Gen. King has notified me that there are certain naval guns and that we can have to place on road blocks and beach positions, some have wheels and some will have to be placed on wooden skids as they are on pedestals. General Parker has approved my allotment to the different divisions and General Parker has been promoted. I have recommended Searight, 51st Division, and Moore, 41st Division, for colonels. Scott and Babcock for lieutenant colonels. Wilson, G-1, tells me I have been recommended by Gen. Parker to be a colonel. Quite a to- do about an order from USAFFE placing the self-propelled mount battalion to defend the roadblocks. Only I am very much against this order. Finally, Gen. King, at my request, protested to Gen. Sutherland; C. of S. The order has been modified to bring Babcock some freedom of action. Field artillery has been placed to cover all possible landing points except in the vicinity of Atimonan. I am a little worried about this sector. Will look it over as soon as possible. The movement of all guns of the 86 F.A. [Philippine Army] has been completed. The bombing of the airfield at Batangas justified my orders to change the positions of the guns there. They were still in position the day the field was first hit. Some of the P. A. guards were casualties.

December 20

At last, I have run down Lt. Col. Pat Searight. He is the same old Pat, a fine officer. We spoke of our days at the Field Artillery School and of his reply to the personnel officer. When asked if he wanted service over here, he replied that he had no desire to be on the inside of a barbed wire fence with the Japanese on the outside. We had a good laugh and a drink and then to the problems at hand. He is going to train his battalion which has no guns as infantry and for replacements. I am going to try and get him some trucks that he needs and some other equipment.

December 21

Lt. Berry; 86th field artillery [P. S.] who is liaison officer from his battalion to south Luzon Force, with his sergeant and all the staff, have accompanied me on an all-day reconnaissance to Atimonan. When we went via Santa Cruz and returned by way of Lucena. We had a fine trip, beautiful day. It's hard to realize that a war is going on right on this island. We had lunch at a little hotel at Atimonan, warm beer, soup and salad. After lunch, to reconnoiter gun positions. The IF is- can we get the guns? On our way back, I was glad to see that the zig-zag over the ridge is prepared for demolition. If the road is blown it should be easy to hold. Back late at night. Conferred with General Parker. I recommended the immediate request for two guns to cover the bay at Atimonan. I am to go to USAFFE to ask for them tomorrow. In the interim, I've ordered Major Lightfoot, 86th field artillery, with a detail to go to Atimonan and survey the positions that Berry and I selected.

December 22

Major Bennett, G-4, accompanied me to Manila. He had some things to attend to there. When I arrived at General King's office, Col. Quintard was there discussing the organization of the 301st field artillery [P. A.], 155 guns [GPF] and two 155 Howitzers. The latter are the ones I want to use to close our back door at Atimonan. My request was turned down. Bennett and I went to the Army & Navy club for lunch. Air raid alarm for about 2 hours. Cavite bombed. We could see it all from the club. I reported to General Parker my conversation with General King and staff. It was decided that I will again go to Manila with the same request in the morning.

December 23

I will never forget my meeting with Gen. King and Col. Williams. I reiterated my request from the day before; gave all of my reasons and arguments. It was a long silence. Williams look to Gen. King and finally said 'no'. I asked if that was final. He replied that it was. I left to report a Gen. Parker. On the way back to Binan, I stopped at a grocery and purchased some canned tomato and orange juice which came in handy later. Major Lightfoot is surveying the positions at Atimonan. It may be that I will ask permission to move at least one of Scott's guns to cover this sector. When I arrived at the C. P. at Binan, I learned that the Japanese have landed in force in Lingayen Gulf from Damortis to Bauang, 80-90 transports with naval escorts.

December 24

The Japanese landed in force at Atimonan and Mauban early this AM.; 40 to 45 transports at Atimonan and 8 at Mauban. Our troops in south Luzon are now out of request for air reconnaissance. Had been denied by USAFFE over Pollilo Island on December 23rd. The plane dispatched on December 22nd had not returned. About 10:00 AM General Parker notified me that his headquarters had been relieved as south Luzon Force and designated as Bataan Defense Force and General Jones now commanding general of the 51st division would take over the South Luzon force. The defense plan; W.P.O.-3, has been put into effect. [This plan provides for the holding of the Bataan peninsula and the fort of Manila Bay until reinforcements arrive.] General Jones has no American officers on a staff to assist him in the operations, so Lt. Col. S.C. MacDonald [infantry], Capt. Arthur G. Christensen and myself are to go to S. Luzon Force to act as his staff. We packed our things and with good wishes and good-byes, leave just after lunch for Santo Tomas where the 51st division has its headquarters. General Jones was at his headquarters and gave us a warm welcome. MacDonald is to act as Commander of Staff, myself as G-3 and all as of the remainder of the General and Special staff; Lt. Berry; 86th F.A., [Philippine Scouts] is with us as 86th F.A., still in our sector. Our troops are 51st Division [P. A.] consisting of 51st Inf., 52nd Inf., 53rd Inf., 51st F.A. with 1 battalion with 75 mm British, 2 battalions as infantry, 51st Division special troops.

-1 division P.A./ 1st infantry only.
-2 battalions, 4 Btry./self- propelled mounts less.
-1 gun battery/ Lt. Col. D.S. Babcock
-1 Co., 94th tank battalion/ Capt. Moffett.
-86th F.A. battalion; 3 batteries, 2 guns ea.,

-155 GRF, 1917 [before leaving Gen. Parker's Hdqtrs.]

I've received orders from USAFFE by phone [Colonel Marquat] to send the tractors; ten- ton prime movers, six in all to Bataan, and to destroy the 86th F. A. guns. I told him that the tractors and drivers would leave at once but that I would not destroy the guns. That, by hook or by crook, I would get them out. [see statement of Lt. A.F. Perkins- junior addenda.] The 41st Division which has been in position on our right has been ordered to Bataan and is now in the process of withdrawing. Our remaining troops, except the one battalion of the 52nd Inf. with detail of 51st division Eng. which was cut off in south Luzon were disposed as follows when the enemy hit: 52nd Inf. less one battalion, Atimonan and along the road between Atimonan and Pagbilao, 53rd Inf., beach defense: Tayabas Bay; 51st Inf., less one battalion, beach defense: Batangas Bay, one battalion in reserve at Lipa, 51st field artillery, one battalion with guns: Tayabas Bay, 2 battalions as infantry - same sector. 86th F.A.; 1 battalion with two guns in position: Nassugbu; two guns covering Balayan Bay [East of Taal]; 2 guns covering Batangas Bay; self-propelled mounts had been ordered to N. Luzon Force; 1st P.A. , less 3rd battalion, Mauban; and 1 Co. of tanks, Santo Tomas. The enemy landings had been made early in the AM. First strength- Atimonan: 1 Dn., Mauban: 1 combat team. Our green troops with no artillery support had broken and retreated in disorder. In the Atimonan sector, the enemy tanks had moved immediately on Lucena attacking our troops at Malicbuy who retired in disorder to Pagbilao where the bridge demolition prevented further advance. Demolitions on the zig-zag vicinity of Quezon Park were not executed as the holes had been ordered not loaded by USAFFE. Trucks with dynamite were on route when they were attacked by aircraft. Strafed and bombed and finally exploded by fire and from enemy tanks as they approach the area

The Colonel's Way

to be loaded. The troops at Mauban had been hit at 1:00 AM, [1st P. A. Inf., less three battalions, at Tignuan]. Routed and retreated in disorder. Col. Babcock SPM battalion had been intercepted from Manila and return to our control. [less 1 Btry.]. General Jones read to us our directive from USAFFE; *"To harass and delay to the utmost the advance of the enemy."* One battery of S.P.M. ordered to Atimonan, 1 battery to Lucban and 1 battery to Tagaytay. Such was our position after lunch December 24, 1941. Orders were issued to troop commanders to carry out our directive, [F.O. #1- SLF; Dec. 24, 1941] to establish a line at Pagbilao. It was just about dark when all orders were completed we stopped to get a little to eat. The kitchen had been moved to the rear so sandwiches and my canned juices were all we had. We split the night between the American staff which puts us on duty about 18 hours a day. My darling- what a contrast to our many happy Christmas Eves. We are in a blacked-out room in a Philippines camp, maps all around, the plans for further movements if the enemy does this or that. Will our troops stand and fight? That is the question. I dream of you and our boys and wish you a happy Christmas. God bless you and keep you this Christmas Day. I do not know how long I slept, it is early. I find that our first P.A. infantry that was routed at Mauban was recognized and with the help of one battery of Babcock's S.P.M.s made a stand at Sampaloc. Two of the S.P.M.s were knocked out, one got out and one was lost. The troops from Atimonan were rallied behind the demolition at Pagbilao. The S.P.M.s destroyed two enemy tanks without loss. General Jones left early to inspect the lines. Pagbilao front was quiet, but later in the day the line was hit and fell back to a new position three kilometers east of Luzon , Tayabas. On the left, or Mauban front, in the late AM or early PM the troops were hit in the vicinity of Piis. One platoon of tanks was ordered forward by Major Rambough over the protest of the company commander. Contact

The Colonel's Way

was made at top of the zig-zag; all tanks were lost. Troops withdrew in disorder towards Pagsanjan. Part of this force was rallied by General Jones and a line formed east of Lucban. Major Rambough was relieved and Major McKee with a small detail of scouts,[some retired, all from McKinley], was placed in command. General Jones had a close call there. One of the half- tracks belonging to the tank company offered to show him the front. He followed in his Ford. Suddenly the enemy opened up with light and heavy machine guns. The half-track crew returned with 30 and 50 caliber. General Jones and driver hit the ditch. The half-track crew maintained its fire. General Jones' driver had jumped in the car and turned it around. The General jumped in and they got out. They half- track was lost but the crew got out with all its weapons. They were all decorated. First battalion, [P.A. Inf.] with Capt. Mendelson commanding at Tignuan, bombed and strafed. No contact. We are really grateful to the tank company. All we had to eat was a large turkey which was extra in the company. It lasted all day and there was some left for tomorrow. Many times during the day I took reports or issued orders over the phone with a hunk of turkey in my hand. What Christmas? I am thankful that my loved ones are safe. Merry Christmas, my love, good- night!

December 26

Headquarters, S. Luzon Force; still at Santo Tomas, [north Luzon Force, Mangatarem Tayug.] We were bombed today. Most of the bombs fell in what had been the special troop area. A lot of the bombs were duds. Rather a funny feeling to hear the bombs whistle and then hear no explosion. Our troops on our right, or south flank, first withdrew to Lucena where the bridges were blown. A stand was made there until late afternoon, after being bombed and strafed and brought under heavy mortar and small arms fire, they withdrew to Sariaya. On our left, or north flank, a line was established between Lucban and Luisana approximately on the boundary line of Tayabas and Laguna provinces. One battalion of 1st the P.A. Inf.; [Captain Mendelson], after executing road demolitions near Infanta, retired to the vicinity of Famy and established a line east of Famy and south of Pagsanjan;   no contact. Lt. Col. Young, who was south of Atimonan, was cut off when the enemy landed and arrived at Santo Tomas. He had a bad time, no food, made his way through swamp and jungle. I was coming off my staff truck and at 4:00 AM, Young, who is a great talker, had just turned in. He started to tell me his experiences. He was still talking when I went to sleep. Had a good meal with Babcock at his C. P. just across the road, scotch and all. Some of the 86th F. A. came by on its way out. Someone,[P.A.], suspected tanks and yelled the alarm. Some of our headquartered troops jumped into the slit trenches and started to shoot in all directions. We had a bad few minutes before we got them stopped. On December 23rd all spare tractors, three, ordered by USAFFE turned in. They were loaded at Batangas the afternoon of December 24. Then came orders for all, [entry December 24th], four were loaded and shipped from Batangas, the remainder were sent over land by marching. This left me without any means to move out the guns and after my statement to Marquet, I began to look for some means to make good. Upon inquiry, Captain Christiansen said he knew a Mr. Perkins, a polo player nearby, who he thought could help. I had prior to this time ordered Scott to begin to get his guns out of position and started for the road by any means in hand, which he had done. Major Lightfoot had been sent to Nassugbu with instructions to get tractors from Roxas Estate and to get the battery there. Started toward a position on Tagaytay Ridge, [left Nassugbu, PM the 25th, occupied new position 1 hour after daylight the 26th]. Christiansen had talk to Perkins on

Christmas Day and at my request had promised to load for tractors on a flatcar at Calamba which he did. Christiansen then called USAFFE for an engine, only to find that they had countermanded their order and promised to return four tractors to Batangas to get us out. He called Perkins back to ascertain if he, Perkins, had seen anything of the engine and the car with the tractors. Christiansen then told him to get the tractors to the main line and to Batangas. About 3 or 4:00 PM the 25th, Perkins came to our C. P. I reported that the train had come in but the crew refused to go any further. He is a graduate of New Mexico Military, and had a rifle in his hand so I told of the use it. The train got to Batangas okay. In the meantime, Scott was having his troubles. Batangas battery was limbered but not on the road by midnight the 25th of December, using three trucks in tandem. Lieutenant Ferrickson [Sam Louis] with one gun without a drawer had, after retrieving his limbers from a canyon, gotten them clear of his immediate position by 6:30 PM, 26th December. We had stopped his tractors on their way out, [telephone], and then they got back to him that night. He passed here at about 12:00 midnight the 26th, one section. His other, without draw bar, was having hard going. [N. Luzon Force line; Camiling-Uningon].

December 27

We moved by echelon today. Our headquarters are again in the Bodie house in Binan where General Parker had his headquarters prior to December 24th. We caught up to the 51st Division, rear echelon, so we eat a little better which is not so good at that. The tank advance of the enemy has been stopped at least temporarily by our bridge demolition. They struck terror into the hearts of our untrained troops, [reference incident at our C. P.] Due to enemy pressure on our south flank, our troops had to withdraw, first to

Candelaria and then in the PM to Tiaong. The bridge on the south road to Rosario was blown. Col. Searight's artillery was emplaced on the high ground on the left of the position, infiltrating the line. The S.P.M.'s,[1 battery],were placed in direct support making this a strong position. The enemy tried to flank the 51st artillery but were driven off. We got our first known enemy casualties. Some information including route map of our proposed advance was obtained. North flank ; no change. Patrol action at R.J. Mauban – Lucban. Enemy returned fire. No attempted advance. One battalion, 1st Regular of P. Constabulary assigned moved two Calamba in resistance. I feel, that if necessary, we can really delay at Tiaong. Our artillery can, until the Japs can bring up their own over the blown bridges, prevent the buildup of the Japs for the attack. Our left as wide open, covered by motor patrols only. Our 1 battery of 155 withdrawing from Tagaytay position; night of December 26th. It gives us some concern. One section of Ferrickson's battery without draw bar finally arrived in Lipa. It is nearly impossible to proceed without a new one. Orders USAFFE is trying to get one for us. [North Luzon line; Tarlac– Cabanatuan.]

December 28

Late last night directive receive from USAFFE to break contact and to keep pace with withdrawal of north Luzon Force. Their location given; Tarlac – La Paz, 91st division withdrawing through Santa Rosa. During the AM our troops withdrew to Aluminos. Colonel Stewart with Reserve Regiment to positions S. of Tanauan, covering both roads. The north flank troops withdrawn to Calauan. The bridge destroyed at Pagsanjuan, one battalion, 1st P. A., Captain Mendelson occupied position behind bridge north of Pagsanjuan. Cabled crossing at Batocan destroyed by Meralco at our request. Our tactics have been unique. We soon found that it was practically impossible to rally our troops for another stand without considerable lapse of time. That it was imperative, therefore, to devise some scheme of maneuver which will not leave the road to the rear open to the enemy. Are units are so mixed that we can no longer call them by their number designation. They are identified by their commanders' names. Our scheme is to place two lines at favorable positions, usually behind terrain obstacles- these behind the front line. When the front line is hit and forced back, the stragglers are collected at the second rear lines, reformed and put in position to form the rear of the third line. Col. Boatright, Col. Young, and Col. Cordere, Commander of the infantry, Col. Searight's artillery: [one battalion with guns, two battalions as infantry], Col. Babcock: the SPM, Col. Stewart, our reserve C.O., has his troop intact. Ferrickson, 86th F.A., had more hard luck. The draw bar was missing was finally replaced by USAFFE Ord. in Lipa, but his limber wheel hit a roadblock near Tanauan in the dark and the gun can no longer be towed. We have called for help from the ordnance. About 8:30 PM I had a call from USAFFE that there were reports of seaplane landings at the Laguna de Bay. The General and C. of S. were in Santo Tomas. I alerted a battalion Constabulary at Calamba and sent the tank Liaison officer and some P. A. officers and men to investigate. Prepared the C. P. for defense and waited. All proved false. The reports persisted until 4:00 AM. Each had to be investigated. [North Luzon front line: Bamban – San Miguel]. Report received from Ferrickson, 86th, his gun cannot be repaired or proceed by marching. We have requested flatcar and engine; will load and ship to Bataan. As to Lightfoot's battery,[Nassaugbu], his requisitioned tractors finally played out on him with the aid of Q.M., Manila. He finally procured two trucks with pintels and proceeded without incident to San Fernando and then to Bataan.

December 29

Headquarter; South Luzon Force, Fort Wm. McKinley troops. Colonel Stewart in position, south of Tanauan. Col. Boatwright withdrew night of the 28th -29th to San Fernando. Passed to control; North Luzon Force. Col. Cordero withdrew same night to Alabang- Pasig line. Reg. of Constabulary ordered to occupy right of line San Antonio – Los Banos. Major McKee's McKinley detail, Scouts and 1st P. A. Regiment, [less one battalion] occupy left of line. Capt. Mendelson with one battalion,[1st P. A.] ordered to Taytay. Prov. Brig. of Constabulary [Gen. Grandcisco], assigned and ordered to take a position west of Tagaytay. Protect the left flank. Position occupied night, December 29th. Col. Cordero ordered to San Fernando tonight a pass to control North Luzon Force. I had my closest call of the war, the night we move the Command Post from Binan to McKinley. The C. Of S. and I remained Binan. The General and Christiansen went ahead to McKinley and called back that we were in and established. It was very late driving without lights. We cross the railroad near McKinley. The train, also without lights, came so close to our car that I could feel the heat from the engine. I don't want any more like that! [North Luzon Force; Bamban – San Miguel, 91st Division; no report].

December 30

It was 4:00 AM when I went to bed. I remember talking to the General and drinking some find old sherry I had in my trunk. Not much, if any, sleep. Christiansen went to Manila. I sent a radio too you, dearest. I hope it got through. It may be the last word I can get to you for a long, long time. Colonel Stewart withdrew by marching, night of December 29th - 30th to San Antonio line, then by truck to vicinity of Fort McKinley. Directive received during the AM to hold line until ordered to withdraw. We are going to use the Los Banos – San Antonio line to cover the organization of a line from Alabang – Las Pinas. The orders have been issued. I did not have a chance to go over this position as I did the San Antonio line. Christiansen returned late. Manila has been declared an 'open city.' We have authority on Perkins, 2nd Lieutenant of Infantry. I have arranged for boats from the Navy to patrol the Laguna de Bay to keep the Japanese from turning to our left. Late PM we received orders from USAFFE two withdraw at once to Bataan. General Jones, absent on inspection. The C. of S., Christiansen and I got orders to the troops, Los Banos – San Antonio line to withdraw tonight to Alabang–Las Pinas. So will the Constabulary Brig. and then night of the 31^{st,} to Bataan. Christiansen and I are in an old taxi leaving just before midnight for Plaridel where we are opening our Command Post. We go by Manila so we can eat. First to the Army and Navy club but it is closed. Then to Tom Dixie's kitchen. A dive but clean. We have turkey sandwiches, beer and ice cream. The place was full of drunks of both sexes. We leave at 2:30 AM. We arrive at Plaridel and open our Command Post at 4:00 AM in a small school house called McKinley and telephone the General we are set up. Check into USAFFE and wait. Stewart is on route due to arrive soon.

December 31

It was just getting light when a staff officer from the north Luzon Force came into our command post. General Jones and the C. of S. had not arrived. This officer asked if we knew the location of the north Luzon Force in that sector. It seems that on the 29th - 30th, the 91st Division P.A. had been routed in the vicinity of Santa Rosa,[route #5] and its whereabouts were unknown. N. Luzon

Force to cover this flank had withdrawn the 71st division P. A. from the line, brought them through Calumpit and sent them north on Route #5 to take position to cover the crossing of the Pampanga at Calumpit and allow for withdrawal. Christiansen went forward with him. Returning later with a report that the line was established at Baliuag. We held Col. Stewart's regiment in Plaridel to constitute a reserve. Later, after the General arrived, we both took a little nap to clear the cobwebs. Placed a battalion of Stewart's command astride the road north of Plaridel to back up the 71st. During the morning General Wainwright, NLF, and G-3 arrived and issued to General Jones in affect the following order: "You will assume command of all of my troops south and east of the Pampanga River and cover the withdrawal of the troops from south Luzon. After the withdrawal of all of your force, you will withdraw the remainder my force across the bridge at Calumpit." General Stephens,[Philippines Scout officer in my class at Leavenworth], 91st Division, came in. He had rallied his men near Baliuag. General Selleck withdrew into Bataan. During the early afternoon we sent in a company of tanks. They had a lively scrap with the enemy in the town of Baliuag. Lost one tank which got stuck in the river, eight of the enemy were destroyed. Twice during the day before the tanks went in, our line gave way but were rallied. During the AM we received orders to withdrawal all troops remaining in the south at once and not to wait for darkness. This was done. I sent Perkins to check and reported me. When they had cleared Manila area, returned about 9:30 or 10:00 PM. All clear. Late in the afternoon, we sent in the S.P.M.'s to shell Baliuag until dark; this, of course, timed with the tank withdrawal. Once, during the afternoon, the schoolhouse in which we had our Command Post was M.G. I was talking to USAFFE G-3. Of course, I dropped the phone and started for the ditch. But when the

The Colonel's Way

General and I got to the door, which was small, simultaneously and there we stayed. Luckily, no one was hit and I returned to finish my conversation. Just after supper time, for we had nothing to eat all day, Colonel Joe Sullivan came through with the last of the troops from McKinley. He gave us a can of peaches and the local priest gave us some warm beer. A little later with a good feeling that all our troops cleared except one battalion of Stewart's which was covering us,[command post], I asked the General when he wanted to close and move to Bataan. He replied; 12:00 AM. I stretched out on the concrete porch and with a wish for a Happy New Year to you, my dearest, and our boys, I was soon asleep. I awakened at 12:00 AM sharp, woke the General and staff. We closed and left after Stewart's battalion withdrew. They were fired on once as they left. We proceeded unmolested to the bridge at Calumpit where the General stopped to be sure all troops were clear. Christiansen and I went on into Bataan to see that the troops were in the positions assigned by the Bataan Defense Force. On our way out, our taxi folded so we pushed it off the road and after removing the distributor, had left it with the driver. I made my way through San Fernando and Lubao, both in flames from bombing. Finally, around 4:00 AM, I came across the Bataan Defense Force. Found the area for our troops. Got fruit juice in the mess and left. It was dawn when I got back on the main road. It was crowded with buses full of Philippine Army. At one place I had to clear a traffic jam with the aid of my pistol. I finally reached Lami where the S. Luzon Force was assigned a bivouac area and did what I could in getting the troops in and under cover. The General came in about breakfast time and we bummed a meal from Col. Cordero. I finally got my bedding and turned in. I had had no sleep for nearly four days.

January 6, 1942

We stayed in the bivouac area in Lami three days, during which time our Constabulary troops were detached and sent to the rear area on beach defenses. I also lost all I had except my bedroll and shoulder bag. My locker was captured in San Fernando. It was on a train that was behind an ammunition train which was hit by a bomb. By the time the ammunition stop going off, the enemy was in the town. On the 3rd, I went up and reconnoitered a route in and that night the 51st division, P. A., moved up on the Abucay line, our main battle position. It occupied the line from the Hacienda west to the Corps boundary; 41st division on our left and the 45th Philippine Scouts on their left. Our position is up in the foothills and mountains. So bad that we have to have a pack train to supply us. It is terribly hard to find ones way in the mountain jungle. Perkins started out with a loaded train and after 2 to 3 hours march found himself back where he started. I received orders on the afternoon of the 5th to return to General Parker's command in my old job as Chief of Artillery. Early this morning, I left believing that his headquarters were in Lami. I went there to find that they are to move on the 7th. I called Bennett, G-4, who sent a car for me. Our designation is now 2nd Philippine Corps, our sector the east side of the Bataan Peninsula. I arrived at headquarters to find that my place, while with General Jones, has been taken by USAFFE Artillery Headquarters: Col. E. C. Williams in charge; two colonels, one major, and a captain. I also find that our governing force at Colis, [26th cavalry, 31st infantry, 71st division] 1st battalion, 88th F.A. [P.S.] 23rd battalion, F.A. [P.S.] 71st F. A. was hit and looks like it will not hold. This was about the middle of the afternoon. I checked Williams' artillery, annex to the Corps, order to occupy and defend the Abucay line which G-3 wanted at once. I made one change, i.e.; I ordered 41st Division so to emplace their 2.95

The Colonel's Way

Howitzer Artillery that they can cover. The 51st division front as Searight's battalion is equipped with 75 mm British which are no good in that type of country. As to the position at Colis, I was surprised that there was no medium artillery, of which we have sufficient, was backing up this line. Just about dark, the General asked me for more artillery to replace the 23rd battalion, [P.S.], which had lost its guns at about 3:00 PM, could be moved up to cover a counterattack at dawn. I was sorry to have to tell him- no. We cannot occupy after dark and fire w/o daylight reconnaissance.

January 7

We moved the Command Post today to Lami and the officers from General Kings Office left, my staff now is one Scout sergeant and me. I've checked the positions of the artillery to defend the new [Abucay] line and am getting a situation map going. Orders to the 301st and 86th [Med.] to keep the road under fire day and night. [East road from Hermosa south.]

January 10

The Japanese are in contact. I had a Major Kerr sent to me as assistant but I am afraid he won't do. He has been asked for by G-3 and I'm going to let him go. Some trouble with USAFFE Artillery about the expenditure of ammunition. I finally convinced them that if we continue to our present rate, which is excessive, we would have enough for six months. Our guns will be nearly worn out by that time. Our Sandy's birthday. How happy we were when he arrived and what a fine boy he is. He has been in my thoughts all day as you are, dearest, every day. An extra prayer for our oldest; may he be a joy to you, dearest. If I do not make it through, I am sure he will.

January 16

I have been quite sick. But back to work again. I am still alone. No staff. I go to bed with the phone which rings many times at night with requests for artillery support. The other morning, I was called by the Brigadier. The enemy was shelling the 41st Division front very heavily. I finally got through to the 301st [Quintard]. We had the Japanese pretty well located on that front so we let them have it. I lay in my cot and listened to the 301st open up. As their fire increased, I could hear the Japanese Artillery die out. Nice feeling. I went back to sleep.

January 19

Down again and our position at Abucay looks bad. The Japanese are coming through the mountains where we cannot reach them with our artillery. I sent all the medium Howitzers we have, 2 [301st], to that flank. We need more. I had Col. Ives, Brigadier C. O., in to confer about position to support the next battle position.

February, [no date]

I've just returned to the Corps Headquarters, which has moved since I went to the hospital. It is quite a long story. Just about the time of my last entry, I developed a severe pain in my right side. Major Drummond, our surgeon, became alarmed and took me on a stretcher to the road and then to Hospital #1 at Lami. I stayed overnight, and feeling better, talked to the doctor into letting me return to duty. I stayed just 24 hours, when the pain hit me again, so back to the hospital. I went this time to stay. In less than 40 minutes after I arrived, I was in the operating room having my appendix removed. I had a local and conversed with the surgeon,

Colonel Atimo, during the operation. I learned later that I had a chronic, not an acute, attack with severe adhesions. For I was quite ill for two or three days after, I have a hazy recollection of General King and staff calling to see me while I was having my stomach pumped out. On the third or fourth night after my operation, the hospital had to be evacuated due to the Abucay line giving way. Its left flank was turned and our troops withdrew to the Pilar – Begal line, night of January 23. This put the hospital within artillery range so we had to move. I was moved on a stretcher in a bus, not a bad time as I was full of morphine. The patients in #1 Hospital were sent to #2 Hospital and the hospital in Little Baguio was redesignated Hospital #1. I went to Hospital #2. Entirely out of doors accept tents for the operating rooms. I was placed in the officer's ward with about 175 – 200 sick and wounded. The medical and nursing care is a marvel of efficiency, but the food was bad beyond description. We have been on two meals a day since January 1. And although food is scarce, there is no excuse for the way it was prepared and served. The sanitation is very bad. Before I was discharged, I got a very bad case of diarrhea. Thanks to my friends Bennett, from our headquarters, and Joe Sullivan and a fine young captain from the 31st infantry, Tom Bell, who lost a leg it Abucay who has the bed next to me, I do not have to depend on the hospital fare alone. He shares what his friends bring him as I do with him. Just what day I came back to headquarters, and now at Lami, I am not sure but it was before February 22, as I listened to the President's speech that day. I must've been terribly thin for the General took one look at me and told me to take a month off and get well. I understand General Marshall, Deputy Commander of Staff USAFFE, who I saw the day I left the hospital, after taking a look at me, investigated the hospital food situation. Although we're on two meals, I have tea and toast if there is any bread at noon. Again- I lost all my things.

All the clothes I had with me at the hospital were left when we evacuated #1 and what I had at Corps Headquartered in it in my bedroll were stolen while I was in the hospital. Everyone is very kind so I have enough to get along with at present.

March 14

I have stayed close to Corps Headquarters in an effort to regain my strength. Things are rather quiet. Artillery and patrol action on the front with spasmodic bombing of the rear areas. Colonel Dougherty has been put in my place in artillery. He was C. of Staff when I left for the hospital. General Funk is now C. of S., a fine officer. I knew him in Hawaii. I have been undecided as to what to do. I understand that my promotion was held up by the Q.M. because I had accepted the Artillery Command in the 2nd Corps. After talking to General King, I decided to take a trip to 'The Rock' and see General Drake, USAFFE Q.M. He was very nice and promised to give me a job. To date, no job. General Parker called me and asked me to take command of the Headquarter detail at the Corps. He said he knew that the job was not up to my rank but the Headquarters was being run very badly and that he was worried about its safety. I was very glad to get the job for, although I am not fully recovered, I am fed up with nothing to do. General MacArthur left for Australia on the 10th. It has a very ominous sound. General Wainwright is to command Luzon Force [Army], Parker -2nd Corps, Jones -1st Corps, Moore- Harbor Defense. I went up to Joe Ganahl's command post to dinner. Had a grand time: cocktails, corned beef, green papaya. He has a fine group of officers who have all been in a lot of action. Our rations have been out again. One item strikes me. The allowance of canned salmon is now one 14 oz can per 100 rations. Ed Williams has offered twice to get letters out for me by sub. I hope that you get them. Both had notification of additional insurance that I had taken out with the government, $10,000 straight life. General Funk has gone to Luzon Force, [Army], to be C. of S. We now have Colonel Steele who was in command of the 31st infantry as Chief of Staff - 2nd Corps.

March 21

Headquarters: Luzon Force, Bataan. A week ago, little did I think that I would be at Luzon Force Headquarters on the Commanding General's Staff. General Wainwright was promoted to Lt. General and placed in command of the U.S. Forces in the Philippines under MacArthur. Wainwright now commands from his headquarters on 'The Rock'- Visayian Force: General Chenoworth, Mindanao Force: General Sharp, and Luzon Force: [largest] General King, and Harbor Defense: General Moore. Late in the afternoon that General King assumed command, Ed Williams called and asked me if I would like to come down and be on General King's staff. I, of course, accepted. So here I am. I found upon my arrival that I was ordered here as G-4 and reported to General King only to have to tell him upon inquiry that the present incumbent is senior to me. General King intimated that he would find some other job for him and I am to be the G-4. I reported to the C. of Staff; General Funk. It is nice to be with him again. He talked to me some time on the status of supply, especially food and gasoline. I am to coordinate the issue of these two items so that the little supply we have of each will, if not replenished, run out at the same time. It is roughly estimated to be April 15.

March 27

All indications are that the enemy is building up for an offensive against us, increased air activity and increased artillery fire. Our G-2 reports landing of additional troops at Subic Bay with lots of traffic in and out of the port. Our foreword observers also report many truck columns on both the east road and a parallel road west of it. It appears that the main effort is building up in the sector generally on the left flank of the 2nd Philippine Corps and between the 1st and 2nd Corp. This, I believe, is typical of Japanese tactics. They will under any given situation attack with terrain rather than troops. This was true of their attacks at Lingayen and Atimonan. We are well fixed. Sleep in the open under shelter tents in a cleared space in the jungle. Have a small shack with lights for night work and a screened mess hall. The food is very poor, not as good as 2nd Corps. We had oatmeal for breakfast, no milk but sugar. For supper, rice and gravy was some boiled green leaves. We did have some vinegar for the leaves. I have been recommended by the General for promotion. I hope this time it sticks. Lieutenant A. L. Collier, a Norma, Oklahoma boy, is G-3. We are great friends. It is nice to have some common topic of conversation. I see a lot of Ed Williams. He is C. of Artillery of General King. Not so long ago the Japanese sent us an ultimatum to surrender. Our failure to answer has been answered by the build-up for the attack.

April 3

Things look rather black. The attack which has been building up has been launched against the 2nd Corps front and, as was expected, has its main effort on the left of the 2nd Corps. The bombing is quite heavy both in at the front and in the rear areas and are lines are beginning to give away. Our #1 hospital was hit by bombs. But with credit to whom it is due, I believe it was not deliberate. The hospital is on the main road with the engineering warehouses on one side and the ordnance on the other. The Japanese apologized over the Manila radio. The food is no better. I am quite thin, but feel quite well, although I did have a bad attack today or so ago. My old adhesions cut up. I had to go to the hospital for an enema and afterwards morphine before I got relief.

April 5

I have just returned from an inspection trip up on the west side: all of the truck parks, gas dumps, all ammunition and rationed distribution points. All of them have suffered from the bombers. I finally arrived at 1st Corps headquarters where I saw a lot of old friends: General Jones, Perkins, his A.D.C., and Bob Lindsay, Chief of Artillery; 1st Corps. He is just the same. Went up beyond the Corps headquarter to visit the ration D. P. with the Corps Quartermaster. The Japanese were shelling the road with two of their 155's that they had captured at Moron. We had to go and return between salvos. I inspected the Corps ammunition dump on my way back. The bombers came over during my inspection. We hit the dirt, but they must have been empty as they dropped nothing. A long talk with other members of the staff. It looks like the end is near. Gasoline is getting short. We are blending aviation gas with kerosene to make something that we can run the trucks on. All diesel fuel is gone so we had to stop work on the air fields. Food, such as it is, we issue about 1/5 American ration by weight, which amounts to about 1200 calories. We all feel that to surrender is the only choice. Our hospitals are crowded was sick and wounded and, at best, without relief. Our food will be gone in less than one week.

April 7

General Funk went to 'The Rock' to confer with General Wainwright last night. His mission, I know. General King has had a terribly hard decision to make and he had made it alone, without any attempt to share it with his advisors, [U.S.]. He is a man of high ideals and great personal integrity. I know it is a bitter blow to him. General Wainwright did the only thing he could under the circumstances, but I will leave that to history.

April 9

Ed Williams, [Col. F.A.] and Marshal Hurt, [Maj. Inf.] went forward at 2:30 with a white flag. We have surrendered. I am, of course, anxious as to all of our futures. Prisoners of War are low forms of beings and no one can even guess what will be our fate. As to our campaign here- I have nothing but admiration for the handful of American officers and men who with poor equipment, an untrained army of Filipinos with worse equipment, totally devoid of air support, held out against an aggressive enemy, who I feel certain had to bring in a second army to knock us out for four months and a day. I believe also that history will prove that it was through our efforts and by our tenacity that Australia was saved for the Allies. No one slept last night. We destroyed our ammunition. I was blown in a dugout by one blast, starting at 2:00 AM and is still tonight. The dump rings our headquarters so we have spent the day undercover. The General with his G-3, Collier, and two aides went forward this AM to meet the Japanese. Just what the situation is, is not clear. The bombers are still at work and all afternoon shells are going overhead. Late this PM, a Japanese captain from the tanks came over to our headquarters. General Funk is with him. I understand that we are to remain here until tomorrow. General Funk after supper was taken as a hostage to Hospital #1 with the Japanese tank company has his headquarters. All firing has died down. The quiet is strange.

April 10

This morning after breakfast we were put in cars. Our baggage limited to two pieces was put in trucks and all taken to Hospital #1. The road was a terrible site; Filipino refugees carrying what they could bring, herded north, Philippine Army and our men being marched to Mariveles – sick, wounded, and the dead all along the road. Japanese Army everywhere; on foot, in trucks, or horse-drawn artillery, pack trains, everything. We hung around Hospital #1 all day. I had a chance and weighed 126 pounds with uniform, pretty thin, no food. At about 5:00 PM we were told to get in our cars. About 12 are 14 in all, as we had been joined by General Weaver,[tanks], and his staff. We were cautioned to keep closed up and started north. The road was a mess. No traffic control. We were constantly stop by a traffic jams. Japanese soldiers would make us dismount, start to search us or take our car. We were saved by our Japanese officer once. I was made to get out with my hand baggage and started for the jungle. I stalled all I could, all that too late. I was rescued by the officer who came back to see what the trouble was. A close call. So passed the early part of the night. We were constantly passing all kinds of troops. About 12:00 AM we arrived at Balanga to where some headquarters were evidently located. Here we were searched and counted. All razors, flashlights, cameras, scissors, nail files, some money, depending on the searcher, were taken. We were given an indication of what our future treatment was to be. Finally, we were loaded up and started again, where to, we were not told. The road, by this time, was deserted and the weather clear with brilliant stars overhead. Had our ride been under different conditions, it would've been a pleasure. Temporary bridges were witness of our efficient engineer troops.

April 18

We arrived here, O'Donnell, Tarlac Province, about 3 or 4:00 AM, April 11th. It is an incomplete P. A. camp which has been both looted and partially burned by the natives. We were counted then lectured by camp C. O., a retired Japanese Army captain. In substance: we are prisoners of war and at his mercy. We are the eternal enemies of Japan. We have no rank, will wear no insignia, we will salute all Japanese regardless of rank. We will be shot if we commit various offenses such as attempted escape, arson, failure to obey and others. We and our things are searched again and again. At last around 4:00 PM, we are taken to one of the buildings and crowded in. Food in the way of rice is provided to be cooked by our men. Thus, the days go by; rice is our only food. Finally, after vigorous protests, we obtained a little salt and finally some camotes and gourds. As our men and officers begin to come in, General King finally arrived. He was put in command and his Adjunct, Halstead, made the single contact with the Japanese. Water is a terrible problem. I finally went to the General to see if something could be done. <u>I got the job!</u> Our men, after the long forced march from Bataan, arrived completely dehydrated. There is but one small pump to supply us and the tens of 1000s of Philippine Army on the other side of the camp. No washing or bathing. We have no razors, so no shaving. It is terribly hot. I try to keep the pump running and finally get the Filipino operator relieved and some good American mechanics put on. I setup priority on the few outlets, put on officer guards, get permission to go to a nearby creek and draw water for cooking,[all must be boiled]. Men stand in line for a hours and leave without water. Our doctors try to get a hospital started, no medicine, buildings with no floors. Our men, weak from lack of food in Bataan, then the terrible Death March up with no food, no water, are dying by scores. What little food we brought is given for the sick. The older officers are pitiful. The end of their long service: POW. Little hope of survival. Some of all ranks and ages just give up and die. God is good. I can eat rice. I can work to keep the water running.

May 1

Conditions have improved a little. Mainly due to our own efforts, the food has been improved by the issue of a little wheat flour. Some native beans and a small issue of coconut oil. About once every 10 days, three or four small calves are brought in. Our strength is about 8000 to 9000 with about 60,000 Philippine Army on the other side. The death rate goes up, still no medicine. The Philippine Red Cross has been refused permission to come into our camp. Why? Our hospital is more of a death house than a hospital. Some of our doctors are like some of our line officers – no good, some are wonderful. Our water problem, thanks to our men and officers, is 100% better. After days of trying we finally have two pumps working both day and night. In this way we can build up a little reserve. Of special commendation are Major William A. Gay, C. of E. [Reg.], U.S.A., for his great work in finding and laying pipe under it almost impossible conditions and otherwise ably assisting me. When the Japs would turn off the water in our camp so they could have enough to take baths, either Gay or I would watch for Japs while the other turn the water on. To Lt. Fred S. Whiteneck, [Temp.] C. of E., U.S.A., and Lt. Lloyd H. Kelsey [Temp] C. of E., U.S.A., in charge of pumps, who kept them running and in repair with nothing. Both of whom, though seriously ill, refused to quit. To these three especially, do American officers and soldiers owe their lives. I thought we were going to lose Kelsey. He was too sick to move. I had to take a doctor out to him on two occasions. We did lose some of our men who with the lack of food, literally worked themselves to death. Sanitary conditions are beyond description. We were issued 10 picks and shovels, then required to turn them in at 4:30 PM. These were to dig latrines, kitchen sumps and bury our dead. Finally, after much protest, we are allowed to keep them. By digging day and night, we can keep the latrines dug, the graves- no. At one time we were 50 bodies behind. The colonels and generals are to be transferred elsewhere. A little extra food comes in via the American truck drivers. It is sold at terrible prices. So far, I have gotten little or none.

May 6

Corregidor has fallen and our flag is hauled down in the Philippines. We feel, or at least hope, that we will be treated better now that the hostilities are over here. Strong rumor that we are to be moved. The dope is out that the generals and colonels are to be moved to Tarlac. As I remember, there are 11-12 generals and about 64 colonels. They leave May 10. Gay and I are in a room in a building used as headquarters. The other night we had our first hard rain. Of course, all the roofs leaked. The Japanese C. O., Capt. Tzuneyosi, came to see if they leaked. Nothing has ever been done about it. Lt. Col. Halstead's, A. G. D., our only contact with the Japanese, actions bespeak his prior service, [enlisted]. He boasted to me that a request was made to the Japanese through him, was in his opinion so ridiculous, that he [Halstead] said nothing to the Japs and reported to General King that they had said 'no'.

May 12

The General and Colonel have left. I feel quite alone. Many of my good friends left. Colonel Sage, CAC, [NG] is in command. I am a little disappointed at his lack of activity. However, we're doing as well as expected, poor food. Our death rate is terrible. Halstead is quite the number one, in his opinion. Made some remark about my going direct to Colonel Sage with something I wanted. I paid no attention to him. Our water problem is about solved, only a question of keeping the old engines running.

June 3

For two days, groups of American POWs have been leaving here for a new camp. They have been told that they have to march to Capas, board a train for a day's ride and then march ten kilometers. The Japanese Corps in charge of the water system tells us the camp is at Cabanatuan. Major Gay and I are scheduled to go this AM. I would not have been able to carry my bedroll but at the last minute we were sent back. Now we are to go on the fourth with the remainder the Japanese consider well enough to travel, but not to walk. Trucks are to be provided – a great break.

June 4

Up at 4:00 AM and placed in groups of 100. At about 7:00 AM, we marched up the hill to the vicinity of Japanese headquarters and were loaded 25 to a truck, exclusive of guards. At about 8:00 AM we left. They are about 100 trucks in this convoy. The system of control was by flag signal passed up and down the column. The rate of the march- very slow, about 25 miles an hour. The day was fine and I enjoyed the trip. We arrived at the camp which is about 9 miles east of Cabanatuan at about 2:00 PM where we were unloaded and counted and finally taken in the enclosure. Lt. Col. Atkinson, [S. O. P.], assumed command of the group which numbers around 2000 to 2100. There were to be more. But at loading time at O'Donnell, the last of the group selected from the hospital were too sick to walk up the hill. Here we were placed 120 in a barrack build for 40. Many of our men are so sick that they cannot control themselves;[dysentery, cerebral malaria]. They have to be segregated. The only building available has no floor. The Japs are no help.

June 6

Col. Atkinson has appointed me Executive Officer. Things are very bad. We are trying to get rosters made, barracks leaders appointed, messes started, the sick cared for, with nothing to do it with. We have placed doctors and medical man with our worst cases which we segregate. The building is horrible beyond description. No water for washing, barely enough to drink, no blankets or other covering. Their clothes are so soiled, that they have to be removed. The death rate is appalling. Many died with no means of being identified.

June 14

We have been here for 10 days and have some semblance of order. We have sent about 500 to 600 to what is to be a hospital. At present, nothing but segregation. How many have died here or on the way? I do not know. It has been a problem to find enough strong to carry the sick. Officers are our mainstay. I have seen many die under the shed where we assembled them. Water is scarce and I have given many his last drink there. Every morning, human filth is all over the area. We find dead in the grass. I found a poor boy, a walking skeleton – no clothes, wandering around the other day. Our doctors try, but there's no medicine. The food is little better than O'Donnell. Still, no meat. We have been allowed by the Japanese to replace our insignia and are to handle the administration of our men. They have also allowed the staff, and later, all officers to purchase limited articles of food. We hope to have this extended to all. This camp is now organized into 3 groups. We are to be consolidated. I hope to keep my job. Work, I believe, is the salvation here.

June 20

We have completed our move and are now Group #1. Col. Atkinson and I have a small room in a wooden building and have to sleep on the floor,[Japanese order]. The remainder of the building contains lieutenant colonels. In the group are Army, Navy and Marines who are separated in barracks and some groups with officers of their own service in command. A small world it is, in search of someone to take charge of our police, a very important job. I came upon Maj. R. L. Ridgley, Jr., U.S.M.C., from Relay, Maryland- a graduate of St. John's. He looks good so he got the job. Things look a little better, although our death rate is terrific. Our purchases are coming in better, a great help. Still, none allowed the men.

June 26

Last night at about 12:00 AM, I was called by the Japanese authorities, taken to an enlisted barracks commanded by Captain Starr, CAG, and told to have a roll call. Three men were absent, one of whom, so I was told by a man that worked in Japanese headquarters, was held by them. Some of our men, due to the heat, had been in the habit of sleeping outside. I complained about this to the Japanese and tried to locate the missing two with no luck in the dark, and the Japanese being very impatient. The man who slept near or knew the missing men, were taken along with me and Captain Starr to a nearby building where they were questioned. I was told that I could go shortly after they began. I arose early and was present at morning roll call. One man,[rumored held by the Japanese], and one other taken after I left last night, were absent. The two who were missing last night were present. A report was made,[routine], to Japanese headquarters and I, Captain Starr, and the two men were ordered there. We waited about 2 hours and were then taken before two Japanese NCOs- Sgt. Maj. Ishikawa, Sgt. Tokumoto, and Interpreter Sekigawa. I was questioned as to where the men were last night. If I had been present at roll call this morning and had witnessed the roll call. I was, for what I could gather, expected to have called the roll in person. The accused were questioned as to their whereabouts the previous night, were told to tell the truth and things would be easy easier on all. That they denied being outside the fence. I argued their case as well as I could but it was evident that the Japanese were convinced that they had been outside the fence last night. The questioning came to a sudden end when two guards appeared, tied the men's hands behind their backs and marched them off. I later saw them in the company of four others tied to a fence in the sun, no hats, in front of the guardhouse. They were shot later that day. I felt that I had failed in my duty in not getting the men off; –[T.E. Hunt, F.J. Reed, R.J. Graham, J. R. Gastelum, I. Penvos, K.L. Sison].

July 1

Our Douglas's birthday, eight years old, time gets by. My Judy, I hope but that this time next year will see us out of Japanese hands. Food and medicine must come or there will not be many of us to tell the tale. Our death rate is still soaring. We lost 776 last month. Dearest, I know our Douglas is having a grand birthday. What would I give to be with you and our youngest today? I love you so.

July 16

I have, through the Lord's Mercy, arrived at my 45th year today. I have said that if I lived through the early part of this imprisonment to see my 45th birthday, I would live to a ripe old age and die in bed in Howard county Maryland with my shoes off. I believe it. Things are better. The Japanese have given us several 100,000 quinine tablets. This is heaven sent and will save no end of lives. The food remains about the same. Our outside purchases are a little better, and as long as my little supply of money lasts, I can eat sardines or corned beef three times a week, which will keep one alive. We have sugar and I had managed one can of tinned milk a week. The mess made me a birthday cake with chocolate icing, made of rice flour. A little heavy but it tasted wonderful. My thoughts are always with you and our grand boys. I hope you are well and happy, darling Judy, enjoying our place in Howard and that you have been notified that I am alive. Next year, I hope things will be brighter.

September 16

We are now well into the wet season with rain every day. Our men have no protection and are obliged to work in the wet. However, we have surprisingly little pneumonia. Diphtheria has cropped up and there's little or no anti- toxin. I was very fortunate in having been given a course a vaccine by one of our officers from Manila. His wife sent it to him. We sent a large detail of men to Japan not so long ago, principally aero and auto mechanics. They are to go into the industries in Japan. Otherwise, things remain about the same, food is still a problem. Our death rate remains high.

September 29

We have just had a terrible tragedy. Soon after the so- called 'attempted escapes' earlier in our imprisonment, the Japanese took steps to prevent further occurrence. Men and officers were placed in groups of 10, so-called 'escape squads'. If one member of the group escaped, the nine remaining were to be shot. We were required to sign an oath that we would not attempt escape. We were required to place a guard inside the enclosure to prevent anyone approaching the fence. At night, a barracks guard was placed on barrack doors to see that no one left except to relieve themselves. We were lectured by Japanese officers, to escape was a crime, mass punishment in the way of ration reductions were metered out. On July 27, about 8:30 PM, Lt. Cols. Briggs, and Breiting, U.S.A., and Lt. Roy D. Gilbert, U.S.N., Res., were discovered crawling down a ditch towards the fence. These men were brought to the American guardhouse, just to rear of the Japanese headquarters. Colonel Briggs was so loud in his protestations that the Japanese ordered an investigation which resulted in the three of them being taken to Japanese headquarters.

I have it on good authority, Briggs continued his protestations in a loud voice, threatening the Japanese with court martial and other taunts. The result was inevitable. They were terribly mishandled, tied up in front of the Japanese guardhouse, where all who passed were required to mistreat them. They were not allowed to relieve themselves and on the morning of the 29th, were taking east of camp and executed. Breiting had to be carried. The small barracks in which Briggs and Breiting were quartered, also the large one were Gilbert was, all remaining were restricted for days to barracks. All extra food taken from them for 30 days. In all barracks all windows and doors were ordered closed at night. An investigation is being carried out on the occupants of both buildings concerned. I hoped no one will be shot as a result of it.

October 8

No one has been shot so far. American Hospital #1 from little Baguio, later, [after we left O'Donnell], has been brought here. It has beds, some medicine, x-ray and real hospital equipment. It is a Godsend. Now, with some little food, many of our men can be saved. We are to have a change in guards and commanders. It is hoped that things will change for the better. Happy birthday, dearest.

October 14

A new ration has been announced by Japanese Hdqtrs. If we get it, it will save many lives. It is rice- 550 g, meat -100 g, vegetables- 330 g, salt- 20 g, sugar -29 g, salt -15 g, tea- 1 gram. It is now definite that our present guards are to leave and that we will be guarded by some men brought here in trained here. The turnover is to be made about the 1st of November.

The Colonel's Way

November 1

We have sent to someplace, [Davao in Mindanao] 1000 officers and men. I was sorely tempted to go, but was told I could not by Col. Atkinson. It is the general belief that more food is available there. We also have also sent recently 1500 officers and men to Japan. All of these were supposed to be technical men of some type. We did not have enough, so the detail was filled out with any healthy men.

November 7

Our camp has absorbed Camp #3 which is about eight kilometres east of here. Lt. Col. Curtis M. Beecher, U.S. M.C., has been placed in command by the new guard which took over November 1. Colonel Atkinson who has been in command of Group #1 has been relieved by the Japanese. A junior major has been placed in command, T. B. Maury III., Class of '34. He has asked me to stay as executive, rather an odd set-up. I talk to Col. Lineback, F. A., who is on camp staff. He urged me to accept. There are many senior officers in our group and he feels that I must stay on for the general good. I've decided to do so. I believe the Japanese are really trying to feed us better. We have built a corral and they're buying many carabaos. We have been told we are to be paid December 1st beginning August 1st.

December 12

We have been paid. Lt. colonels: $280.00 of which we received $30.00 and $60.00[monthly] to be deducted for our board and shelter. The remainder is deposited in the Japanese Postal Savings. We cannot draw against it except in emergencies for eye glasses or special medicines, if they can be purchased. 100 of the senior officers have been allowed to contribute $50.00 each from Postal Savings to a fund known as the Welfare Fund. This fund, administered by us, can be used to buy extra food for the sick and weak. In each group, there's a board who decides which men are eligible. The food is prepared in the mess and issued directly to the individuals on the welfare. It will save many lives. Officers are not eligible. We have percentages set up so that purchasing power is so far is we can, set-up to work. No hardships, i.e. Welfare to purchase all available eggs so that those who put up the money get none.

December 18

A week before Christmas. I can picture so well, dearest, the excitement and anticipation of a visit from Santa enjoyed by our boys, for I know the loving care that their wonderful mother will give to every detail to ensure a wonderful Christmas for them. Someday, my Judy, I will be back to you and then, and only then, will I truly be happy. The Red Cross has managed to get into us some Christmas packages of food. Wonderful! They contain candy, jam, cheese, crackers, tobacco. In some form, milk, corned beef, fish, stew, and sugar, tea or chocolate. We have 2 ½ per. Also, bulk corned beef, sugar, meat and vegetables stew, raisins, dried fruit, cocoa. Enough to last us 3 months. We are going to have a fine Christmas! The food is a gift from Providence and will start many up who have been despaired of.

December 25

Merry Christmas to my Judy and our boys. I slept very little last night. My thoughts were too much of you, and although it was

3:00 AM before I went to bed, I could not sleep for thinking. A wonderful moonlit night. First, we had a fine show with Christmas carols, O.O. Wilson, Lt. Col. [Zero to us], in charge. Then to the barracks where most of the officers from the 2nd Philippine Corps headquarters are, for tea or cocoa and cake, mostly rice, at 12:00 midnight. As it was in front of my house, I went too High Mass. It was <u>impressive</u> with the setting of the bright moon over head. All done in Latin and at no time participated in by the congregation. It seemed pagan to me. I went to communion this morning and for lunch we stuffed on to roast ducks. What a treat! Maury and I went through the barracks. One young soldier, who looked much too young to be here, sick and full of sores, when I asked him if he was getting along all right, he said: "Colonel, this is the happiest day of my life!" I nearly cried. Everyone is optimistic. It is wonderful what a full stomach will do. The last night's some of our rank got a little drunk. I had to speak to them. So ends our first Christmas in prison. Much better than I had dreamed. I long for word of my loved ones.

<u>January 1, 1943</u>

To you, my Dearest One and our boys, may this be a happy and peaceful New Year. I hope that it will also see the close of the war and that we will be united again. More things have come via the Red Cross. Medicine, except what is needed for amoebic dysentery, for which we are in dire need. I cannot understand why it has not it been included, unless it just failed to arrive. Some hats, wool slip-overs, toilet kits, razor sharpeners and shoe brushes,[an ironic gift as there are practically no shoes left and none are issued]. However, we are tremendously better off than we were three months ago. The Japanese are issuing us the ration as published with an additional 50 g of meat for each sick man.

Twice a month, they buy us some type of citrus fruit to prevent scurvy. Usually it is the native calamansi, something like a very small sour orange. We also are being issued 50g of mongo beans in lieu of that much rice. Very welcome. Our men are beginning to show the effects of the food. The rains have stopped entirely. The days, not unpleasantly hot, with cool nights. This will continue until the end of February when it gets hot again. I still suffer from insomnia. Our death rate is dropping, 149 last month. Down considerably but still very high.

February 6

The what a wonderful and complete surprise I received from you, my Dearest and our boys, a message – your Christmas one; the first word I've had for a year! [I got your last Christmas one on Bataan after I left the hospital]. The I believe that you know that I'm alive as at the bottom of the list was a notation: "RE: your list of war prisoners." It is such a great relief to know you and our lads are alright. I hope the absence of word from Mother is not a bad sign. The additional food is having its effect, both that supplied by the Japanese and from the Red Cross. Everyone is gaining weight and our death rate is falling steadily, 72 last month and less than 10 so far this month. Our officers are being required to do manual labor on the farm. The bad feature is the breakdown in discipline, yet the Japanese expect us to administer the Camp. We have protested with no avail. We are, by order, keeping weight charts of each man.

March 19

Dorsey's birthday. We are still doing very well. The Red Cross bulk food is still holding out. Our men are gaining weight. The

Japanese are still doing, I believe, their best to feed us. We are no longer getting beans but we have received fresh tomatoes, onions and a good grade of native greens. The news we get from the papers supplied by our captors does not, in my opinion, indicate an all-out offensive in this sector this year, from what I read. Germany is the number one and all of our effort is being directed there. The Germans, according to the Nippon Times, certainly took it on the chin before Stalingrad. We have had to send more and more officers to do manual labor on the farm over our protest. As the detailing of the individuals is left to us by the Japanese, it has led to some feeling, primarily the system of who is to go and who is not. We try to send no sick men to work. This is complicated by the Japanese who do not recognize our marking of men and officers' quarters. They say if a man is sick, send them to the hospital. This, of course, brings more problems; constant turnover. To avoid this we keep, and I believe rightly so, all who were considered capable of being returned to duty in from 5 to 7 days. Our policy is to send first; all duty officers and men, second; all light duty men, third; light duty officers, and fourth; quarters men. Any shortage is made up from the drafts from S. D. such is kitchen police section. We have had several instances of men refusing to go to work for one reason or another. My policy has been to be very severe with them. As the Japanese allow us to administer the camp, I believe any sign of weakness will lead to their taking over. Men, and I regret to say, one officer, who have refused to obey orders to go to work have been given 'a talk' as to the reasons. If they still refuse, they have [by my orders], been deprived of their food until they go to work.

The Colonel's Way

July 1

The months have slipped by and today is our youngest birthday. Our Douglas must be quite a big lad now. I know that his mother has made his birthday very happy for him. I hope that by the time he is a year older this war will be over. Things have gone quite well, our death rate has dropped until a death is quite rare. The food is not as plentiful as a few months ago but we do quite well. Our greatest worry is to meet the demands of the Japanese for work parties. We are having a lot of brutal beatings by the Japanese, work supervisors on the farm especially. Every case is protested vigorously to Japanese Hdqtrs. but with little or no result. I will admit that in some cases, our men are at fault but in the large majority, they are absolutely uncalled for. Language difficulty is a great contributing cause. I wonder where you are, if at Our Decision for the summer or possibly at Ocean City and if the Plimhimmon was ever sold.

August 12

The rains have started but not to a bad point yet; mostly an afternoon rain. Food is scarcer and prices at the commissary are sky-rocketing. We still receive a meat ration, but not nearly as much as before; dried salted fish has been issued in lieu of meat on several occasions. It is hard to get by the nose but it's better than nothing. The condition of the men, although the Red Cross food is all gone, is good. Death rate, way down. Part of the answer is simply that the strong survive. Roughly, every other man who was on Bataan or went through O'Donnell, is dead. Those who came later with the fall of Corregidor fared much better, their losses between 200-250. Recently, the Japanese commander here called upon certain Field officers to write letters containing criticisms of the camp and the general treatment. To my surprise, he called a meeting of all Field officers and read in Japanese a detailed answer to all of the more important and general criticisms. He first explained that Japan was in a war for her life and that all supplies were short. He went on through seven points, explaining to some length that physical punishment was recognized and practiced in the Japanese Army, that the language barrier was a contributing cause. However, he promised to stop the beatings and assured us that all cases would be handled in accordance with their regulations. He finished his talk with the remark that it was his greatest desire to return us to our families in good health at the end of the war. I consider this a definitive indication of change in attitude for the best.

August 28

The rains increasing but still able to do a great deal of outside work. The Japanese inspected the area with the view of moving the hospital from the other side of the road into this area. It is, I believe, an effort to reduce the camp area and to cut down the number of Japanese required to administer and guard us. The Japanese have been insisting that individual cooking stop. This is, of course, a serious blow as we have been cooking beans, meat, coffee, rice cakes, eggs, etc. for individuals in a sub- kitchen built for this purpose. After conferring with Major Kriwenek, our Group Commissary officer, we have adopted a system of group cooking. Twenty-four hours before you want delivery, you place your order for what you require to be debited from your stock at hand and held to your credit. For coffee, we were able to purchase enough to allow straight purchase without prior credits. Recently, certain POWs were given testimonials by the Japanese for cooperation in the running of the camp, Colonel Beecher, the

Adjunct and others. More indications of a change in attitude. I have great hopes that by this time next year, we will not be POWs. Everything is looking very well.

September 8

The hospital is to move into this group. Our staff will be disbanded or absorbed by the other groups. I hate to see this happen. I have been the virtual commander of this group for 14 months and I feel but I have done a good job. The men and officers have responded well and we have come a long way with better spirit, health, sanitation and general welfare. I will not ask for any special consideration from A. P. Hqtrs., but will take what comes.

September 16

Our wedding anniversary, my Judy mine, I have lived the day over today. Please God, may I be with you on our next, never to be separated again and may we celebrate twice over this, are 17th. I got a big lump in my throat when our orchestra played our favorite: *Smoke Gets in Your Eyes.* Remember the nightclub after the party Mother gave us before I left? I was so proud of you, my Judy.

September 22

The hospital moved today. Group #1, as I knew it, is no more. Colonel Beecher has made me Executive, and although it is not recognized by the Japanese, I have something to do and may be of some service to my fellow prisoners. I moved into A.P. Headquarters #3, a small barracks next to the headquarters were the staff lives. Major Maury is to be one of the adjuncts. He is coming into #3 with me. I was able to cash a State's check on our bank in Ellicott City for $100 for which I received P180.00. I now can help some of my friends and buy what is available, which is little. News is still good. Our morale is high.

DIARY TWO

{October 2, 1943- July 13, 1944}

The Colonel's Way

The Colonel's Way

My darling Judy,

As I've said in my other book, which is now about complete, it has been reconstructed from notes that I have kept, and from memory. This was necessary for two reasons; first -during active campaign I was too busy or incapacitated. During our surrender in the early days of our captivity, I considered it too dangerous to put anything in writing which refers to the war or the Japanese. This danger, although still present, is now much less so from now on until the end, which God willing, will unite us, never to be separated again. I'm going to try to make entries as they occur.

Arthur L. Shreve

October 2, 1943

We are in the middle of the wet season and it has rained nearly all day. Too bad that it is the day that the Japanese gave us as Sunday, for had it been any other day, our men ,due to the rain, would've had a day off. I went to church and communion. We have a short service each Sunday. The chaplain is from north east Missouri. Memories, dearest mine, of the times that we have worshiped our God together. So much rain I have been at unable to get my daily exercise cutting wood. I'm quite comfortable in the staff barracks. There are four of us there. I have a spring bed and with my air mattress that I have managed to hold onto, I am quite comfortable. Food is falling off and although I have some money there is little that one can buy.

October 6

Weather improving. For three days the Japanese have had 300 of our officers appearing in a movie, the title being "Down with the Stars and Stripes." Our men are in the scene depicting the fall of Bataan and Corregidor. It is better than the farm. My health is remarkably good considering the diet. I still have some sugar to go on the morning 'lugao'. None has come into the camp officially. I have been able to get some on the black market for P5.00 a canteen cup. The commissary prices are going up. Eggs- 26¢ each, bananas - 4¢ each, Guava jelly –P$4.70, 1 pint jar juices- P$4.00, chicken- P $3.75, S. Pancit- 80¢ per canteen cup, oranges – 30¢ each, beans we cannot get, coffee 2 pounds –P$12.75. Have cut wood for about an hour. Had my bath, and soon, supper and a show by the Camp band.

October 8

Many happy returns of the day, dearest Judy, and may I be there next year to be happy with you. In church I said a special little prayer this morning, you are always in my prayers and in my thoughts. But this was a special one for you on your birthday. I've had a very happy feeling all day that you and our lads are all well and as happy as can be under the circumstances and that it will be not be too long before the war will be over. So many times, Judy mine, have I felt that I must just get through this for there are a lot of little things that I know I have done. Foolish, selfish things that have made you unhappy. I want to live to ask forgiveness and they will never happen again. The Japanese have ordered us to consider the surplus Medical personnel over and above a maximum which they have set up for the hospital and the groups, [142]. Both doctors and Corps men are available for all work details. I weigh 147.5 pounds, a little light but not bad for the food and the heat. I feel well, so do not worry.

October 10

The exchange ship has left. There are rumors from Santo Tomas where all aliens are interned, that some, mostly English, were for some reason taken from the original list. Applications were made for substitutes, and due to language difficulties, the approval came back for *prostitutes*. The sailing list then had five classes to wit: the Preachers, the Physicians, the Politicians, the Profiteers, and the Prostitutes. The Japanese have levied a tax on all purchases made by our commissary, 3% on the gross. It is to be paid by the vendors to pass it directly to us. This fund is to be used for the good of the camp as a whole when it is has accumulated P3000. The profit that we now have, about P4000, we can spend as we see fit.

October 18

Little or no change. Less rain. The long awaited Philippine Independence was declared with much celebration on the 14th. The J.M.A. is officially discontinued. The 16th saw the Burma offensive start. I've had a cold but it is better. We had a Walt Disney movie on the 12th. Made me homesick.

October 24

Sunday. If Philippine Independence has done nothing else we now have Sunday on Sunday. We started today. I did not get to church, cold is still here but better. Yesterday one of our poor insane men from the hospital disappeared. He was present and taken to the latrine by the Medical Corps attendant just before morning roll call and absent at roll call. He had attempted to kill himself several times. The Japanese have confined the Attendant, the Barracks leader and one of our guards who was on the post where the man was supposed to have escaped. Our meat ration has been very low lately. 45 officers and 57 enlisted have Med. Been sent to Group #1 and #2 for duty, not medical. The weather at home must be grand now. Two years ago tomorrow I had to say goodbye to you and our boys. That, dearest mine, was the hardest thing I have ever done in my life. I will never forget the station, you in the car, and watching you drive off. You were brave. God grant another year will not go by before we are united again.

October 27

Enlisted men involved in or associated with the supposed escape of the insane patient in the hospital, have been placed in the guardhouse some for 20 days and some for 10 – all on heavy confinement, two days out of three on rice and water. They are in our custody. Group Staffs are to be punished upon the occasion of future escapes. We have been notified that we are to receive no more newspapers. My cold is better. I've just learned that Japanese sentries have been put on our guardhouse.

October 30

Our insane man was found on the farm. He was discovered by some Americans lying in a pile of vines and other discarded grass, etc. He was eating a raw camote, very weak, covered with filth and unable to walk. He was brought to the Japanese headquarters on a stretcher where, I understand, he was questioned as to his method of escape. From all accounts he was entirely out of his head. That night Colonel Beecher was called in and notified that the culprit had been treated in accordance with Japanese regulations. My cold is nearly gone. So are the rains.

November 11

Twenty-five years ago today was the end of our last big war. I hope that it will not be long before we see the end of this one. We had some good news last night. The Japanese authorities notified us to prepare a warehouse for Red Cross packages from the States. No one knows how welcomed they will be. We were inspected by the Japanese general who is in charge of POWs here. He brought us some magazines and also reduced the hours of work on the farm. The last escape has resulted in a strengthening of the fence. It is being built higher and it is rumored an apron is to be put on it. Rains continued with very hot interim. My cold is better. With my duties, my wood chopping, and reading a little,[eyes are not too good], the days go by quite fast. It is the nights that are so lonely.

November 14

Sunday, and I did not get to church. I slept so badly last night that I did not get up until 8:30 AM and by that time I attended to a few things it was too late. So many things of late that have brought thoughts and memories. On Friday night, 12th, the Japanese had the best and latest movie we have had, "Look Who's Laughing", Charlie McCarthy, Edgar Bergen, Faber McGee and Molly, made late in 1941. It was in fine condition. I enjoyed it to no end but I couldn't sleep that night. Yesterday we were told by Japanese headquarters that there were individual packages and letters in the Red Cross shipment recently arrived in Manila. And that we must, from our records, make up a list of where the men were so that the things could be sorted. They made available some of their records. I find that to date 5200 POWs have been sent to Japan. That last night we had a recital by the Camp Male Chorus. They sang some lovely songs. So between thoughts of letters from you and fond memories, again- a bad night. I've managed some cod liver oil. I hope that it will help my eyes. Joe Ganahl is outside. We're going to cut some wood for an hour or so. It should help the sleep.

November 19

Typhoon! We have been in one for the last five days. Finally, it began to clear yesterday and today it has been clear but not humid. The first day the wind was from the north and that night, changed to the south and finally blew itself out in two days. It rain over 5 inches, a lot of rain. Lots of buildings were blown down, mostly sheds, but much damage was done to roofs. At one time it looked as if the rain was not falling but going parallel to the ground. Everyone and everything gets wet and stays that way, bedding, blankets, shoes, clothes, all develop green mold, so today with the sun; everything was out to dry. We have further news of Red Cross supplies. We will get about 500 tons according to Japanese headquarters. If they're going to censor the mails, Lord knows when we will get it. I soon will be in the islands two years. A long time to be separated from my Dear Ones. My thoughts are always with you, my dearest, and of the happy days that are to come. So many plans and dreams, may they soon come true.

November 21

Another Sunday and again I did not go to church. This time I was interfered with by a meeting of officers and Barracks Leaders to talk of the old, but ever-present, subject of escape. We, the Americans, are held by the Japanese responsible that none of us escape; a strange system. A check on the meat ration for the past week shows an average of about 50 kilos or 100 pounds of meat and bone for 1,000 men, hardly a subsistence ration, much less a ration for men doing hard labor as ours are. Among the last batch of magazines brought us by the Japanese general was an issue of House Beautiful entitled 'Builders Manual'. I've studied it with great interest for during our incarceration, I had made some sketches of what we have planned to do with their little place in Howard. I have two or more plans, both for our proposed addition and the rearrangement of the present interior. Of course, I think there are good. I spent hours of thought on them. There are some attractive things in House Beautiful that I made some notes of. We can have a lovely place without too much expense; we have such a good start. I'm especially pleased with my plan for the garage and servants' quarters. I can't wait to show it to you.

November 25

Thanksgiving Day. We're not allowed a holiday, however, we all have a great deal to be thankful for. Information has come in by truck driver from Manila that in addition to food contained in the Red Cross packages, including much needed amoebic dysentery medicine for all. Our great and generous nation. It is wonderful to know we have not been forgotten. Our information also indicates that the Red Cross authorities are handling all of the supplies. Due to the typhoon, the railroad to Manila has been out for over a week. It is in again with the first train arriving yesterday. Manila was badly hit by the typhoon. They had a bad flood with a loss to PRTIMCO of 10,000 pesos of much needed supplies and food. Our order with the Bureau of Animal Industry, jam, syrup, vinegar, etc., was also badly hit. We will get it but late. Our own little barracks had our dinner yesterday, roast duck, sage dressing, baked camote, salad and cake. I had so much I was uncomfortable although we ate half at noon and half that night. I inspected the noon meal at one of our messes. They do wonders. Baked beans, [purchased by Welfare], meat and vegetable soup stew, fried greens, cake with ice tea. American money from commissary profit supplied sugar, extra fat, grinder to grind rice flour, and as above, beans. Our meat ration for 23 days this month, averaged as follows:

Date	Issue Kg.	Ration St.	Gr.
1	81	1000	81
2	103	1000	103
3	107	1000	104
4	114	1000	114
5	114	1000	114
6	100	1000	100
7	109	1000	109
8	103	996	103.5
9	105	994	106
10	115	995	116
11	101	994	101.5
12	105	994	106
13	100	994	106
14	0	985	0
15	0	983	0
16	60	990	60.6
17	0	990	0
18	105	989	106
19	71	989	72
20	98	989	99

21	78	984	79
22	63	983	64
23	48	983	49

| Average: | | | 82.4 |

Twenty-two Medical Corps men to duty, not medical. Our hospital is cut way below efficient strength. Sixty men to Manila including four officers; temporary duty. Another 100 men to leave soon. We are to have a service tonight. I will try to attend. Later, our service was very nice, so many came that I had to sit outside. Chaplain Donald spoke. We sang some of our familiar hymns and all went away better for our going. I just remembered; our salad dressing was made with oil from the powerhouse supplied by our captors to run the electric power plant.

<u>November 28</u>

Again I did not go to church. I spent the morning on the wood pile, one of the regular cutters was sick where I usually go to cut in the afternoon for exercise, so I took his place. I certainly got a workout. Red Cross packages have been arriving all day. I must admit that the Japanese are scrupulous in their care to see that there is no looting by their troops. M.P. Guards on all cars and receipts for each package. A great change from last year where there were packages strewn all along the road from Camp #3 to Cabanatuan. It appears that each man will get four packages of about 12 pounds each of much needed food. There also about 600 cases a miscellaneous supplies: shoes, shoe repair kits, toilet articles, phonographs and records, sheets, books, toilet paper, soap, cigarettes, tobacco, pipes, athletic equipment and recreational supplies. There is much excitement among the men and morale is tops. There is mail in Manila. I would trade my packages for a letter from you, my sweetheart. I know you have written but I also know the Japanese. There will be many a letter lost in censorship. I stopped in at a belated Thanksgiving dinner held by one of the enlisted Co. Their C. O., Major Howser, Inf., U.S.A., (Reg.), deserves no end of credit. He collected enough money to buy a carabao [cow], some beans, [I borrowed from all over the camp until his order was filled], coconuts for cakes and sugar for the tea. They had the band. Menu; baked black beans with meat, potatoes, greens, sprouted mongo beans, rice, tea and cake. The band, as usual, played my favorite piece when I arrived.

December 2

The Japanese authorities upon examination of our Red Cross packages found some Old Gold cigarettes with a patriotic verse printed on the package so they opened all of the packages, exposing all of the untinned; [chocolate, prunes, cheese, etc..] to spoilage. They allowed the issue of one package, one more to be given us at Christmas, as they spoke vaguely of making the other two last until April. Colonel Beecher is having some success with the suggestion to give us all of the articles that might spoil at the next issue [Christmas] leaving the canned goods only, in the two remaining. Our hosts have taken from us so far: three cases of cigarettes, 1000 shoelaces, 100 sewing kits, three shoe repair kits, 16 packages of red cross food [taken on the excuse that it is a sample to be sure that the food is okay for us to eat] the miscellaneous athletic equipment. What more will they get on one excuse or another? I got a so called "invalid package": one can of beef, one salmon, two chocolate bars, 3 ¼ ounce butter, ½ pound cheese, two soluble coffee, one Prem., two ham and eggs, two corned pork, one meat paste, eight Bouillon cubes, ¼ pound sugar, 12 vitamin C tablets, 116 prunes, 116 dried milk, two bath soaps; I also received one razor, two packages of blades, one sewing kit, two bars laundry soap, toothbrush, tooth powder, comb and shoe polish. All very welcome. It is all a mystery to the Japanese where it all came from, for according to them, our country is starving and out of metals.

December 6

Went to church yesterday, Communion with what I hope is the beginning of a choir. In the afternoon the Chaplain had a church meeting. We're going to try and have a grand Christmas service. All of us have something to do with its success. I am going to try and make the chapel more attractive. It is hard to have to watch the Japanese playing baseball with what we know came in our Red Cross shipment. 1500 packages of Old Golds taken from our Red Cross packages because they had a verse of a patriotic nature on them, were sent to Manila by the Japanese. We will never see them again. I have another cold, so last night the doctor gave me some aspirin and iodine; result- strange and weird dreams. I was home and, in talking to you, said that it was too bad I had been caught here by the war and if I had been some other place I might have been promoted to Brigadier General, to which you replied, 'you did not think so, that I had been sent here to get me out of the way...'. Then I said, 'let's retire and go to the country,' to which you said; 'No, I want to stay in 10 more years.' I was very upset. We are having cool weather with some rain. I enjoy it. As you know I do not enjoy the heat. I have had to stop cutting wood until my cold is better. Leaves me at loose ends in the afternoons. Our issued food is very scarce, small meat rations, some days none.

December 12

Less than two weeks until Christmas. I know our boys are excited. All I ask from Santa is a letter from my Judy. I've been in bed three days with a cold, felt quite bad but am up again. We sent a detail of 99 men and one officer to Clark Field. We see evidence of increased air activity here. More and more bombers. They seem to be on patrol missions as they fly singularly and in pairs. As the Japanese in issue us no more papers, we get no news except through the grapevine. Our diet, due to Red Cross food, is much better. Food outside is evidently getting very scarce, rice is quoted on the black market at P175.00 a sack. We're quoted a price of P70.00 for a kilogram of 2.2 lb. bag of pepper. We are still getting rain. Very unusual for this time of year.

December 16

The days are fixing by. My cold is quite a lot better and I can cut wood again. A small world we live in, two nights ago I was sitting on headquarter steps when a man came up in the semi- darkness and asked where I could be found. I told him who I was and he asked if my mother lived on Lanvale street in Baltimore. He turned out to be Corporal Schatz, George, 803rd Eng. from Ellicott City, Maryland. He and his father are carpenters and painters. The last job he did before he came in the service was to do over mothers first floor. You remember? He was as glad to see me as I was him. We talked of home and all those things. I told him he could go right to work on Our Decision when we got home. He had just married before he left and has a child. He has never has seen it nor knows if it is a boy or girl. His sight has been impaired by a lack of food. I talked to the doctor about him. He will, we hope, get better with proper diet, but may never fully recover. He is going to come down to see the pictures and plans of the house. Things in camp, just about the same. Rice with a few vegetables is all we get to eat.

December 18

Saturday night before Christmas. Oh dearest, I can imagine the excitement that is prevailing at 502 Wingate Rd. Where is the tree going to be and what is Santa going to bring for Christmas? I certainly hope that Santa brings your Arthur to you next Christmas. I have arranged to get the decorations for the stage for the Christmas services, both the Catholics and non- sectarian. I hope it will look well. Our Red Cross shoes have gone a long way. Nearly every duty man will receive a pair and with the repair kits, we will be able to fix all the shoes turned in, so everyone will get some sort of foot wear. For one mess, about 925 men, the Japanese have issued us 42 kilos of sugar, 150 lb. pail of cooking fat and 100 lb. pail of dried fish, this is an extra issue for Christmas. Col. Johnson, our Commissary Officer, told me today that one of the Filipino vendors asked him today for a pass to get him safely by the guerrillas as he was afraid to go where he was going unless he had it in writing, that the supplies were for the U.S. War Prisoners. That is some commentary on the Japanese occupational force. The weather is fine again, cool and clear. My cold is about gone. Joe Ganahl and I cut wood every day now for about 1 ½ hours. I weigh 150 pounds, a little light.

December 25

Christmas, a lovely day, but first about Christmas Eve. Our show, to have been put on by O.O. Wilson's players was postponed at the last minute due to the arrival of a movie. Japanese supplied first propaganda then the feature; "Top of the Town." Very good, although terribly cut. I think we all enjoyed it very much, lots of singing and dancing. A direct gesture by the Japanese, I believe. After that, the Glee Club sang carols. [Oh dearest, what memories. Specifically, Leavenworth; my waiting for you that wonderful night.] Then at 11:50 PM, Catholic High Mass I had attended last year. So after seeing that the Japanese, who were to attend, were properly seated, I went to bed but not to sleep. I lay there for 3 ½ hours dreaming of you and our lads and of the day's to come after this is over. I forgot to tell that we had our Christmas dinner yesterday noon, roast duck, wonderful dressing, gravy, and of course, rice topped off with fruit cake made of rice flour, raisins, prunes, chocolate from our Red Cross packages for icing. For supper I had a cocktail; real brandy and orange juice. I proposed a toast to our country which was solemnly drunk, standing by. This morning I called on Group Staffs to wish them Merry Christmas, gave some tobacco to two boys from Baltimore, and went to church. I've been trying to fix up the chapel was some results. We had quite a congregation, over 50 for communion. Tears filled my eyes when one of officers recited a poem of Christmas- 'thanks to God for the safety and happiness of our loved ones at home.' I must be off to the hospital to cheer those who are fortunate enough to be there. More later. Colonel Wilson's players gave a fine performance of Dickens Christmas Carol, adapted to the present and to our situation. The carols were sung again. A fine show. We are having trouble getting what I understand are the Red Cross medicines. A list was furnished as of what was available. However, are requisition was turned down on the basis that it was too big. We're now going to ask the Japanese Med. what we can have and requisition on that basis. All this time and we have yet to receive one pill from the Red Cross shipment that arrived in October. I've just talked to the surgeon who informs me but there are among the drugs many that we are in dire need of, amoebacides and vitamins, concentrates being the most needed. Colonel Craig is still trying to get them.

January 1, 1944

Happy New Year, my dearest, to you and our boys. May it hold for you all of the happiness and joy that you wish for. I hope and pray that the coming year will see the end of the war and that we can be united again. Only half of me lives when we are apart. Last night we had a New Year's Eve show. Wilson has worked hard and has done no end of good. His show last night was a cavalcade of bits from the shows he has put on since we came here. The band is now a really fine one employing two arrangers. They played both popular and classical tunes. After the show we went to the Medical headquarters. Colonel Craig served us a hot rum drink made with milk. Very good. We stayed until about 11: 30 PM and with many happy New Year wishes, we return to our barracks to sit and talk until 12 midnight to see the New Year in. Sergeant Mitchel [retired], our chief cook and Major domo, had his 61st birthday today. We had a great dinner at noon for him. A bottle of rum provided us all with a drink to toast his health while the band played Happy Birthday. Roast chicken and duck, candied sweet potatoes of a sort, native greens with garlic vinegar, fine gravy made with bouillon powder from Red Cross packages, rice bread with butter [Red Cross] and fruitcake, rice flour with prunes and raisins [also Red Cross]. For prison camp- a banquet. I feel uncomfortable from over-eating. Supper was impossible although, I cut wood for about an hour and a half.

January 10

Our Sandy is 13 today. Many happy returns to you, our oldest. Your mother and father were very, very happy when you arrived 13 years ago today. I know you have been a joy to your mother during my absence and will still remain so no matter what may come to pass. We are given some Tokyo Times papers covering a few days in October, November, and December last. They are very interesting even if they do claim tremendous losses for our side. We, the Americans, British and Russians, are moving, though slowly. Things are going well with little change. Postcards were given to us to be sent home. No dates, no reference to anyone in camps. No business and many other restrictions are placed on their contents. Weather- clear and cool. We have yet to receive medicines or mail reported in Red Cross shipment. I received my second money from outside. With prices so high it is a necessity. Two checks of $100 each have been drawn on our account at the Patapsco State bank. Meat is still a serious problem. We have had none since before Thanksgiving. Fish dried and salted we do get, and our Red Cross packages will last if we stretch them until March 1st. Our efforts in this connection although progressing satisfactorily, from all reports, have shown no results. I have a comfortable feeling that I will see our Sandy before he has another birthday.

January 15

A little flare- up over our musical program. The Japanese N.C.O. of the day found our band giving a concert in the hospital dysentery area. This area, by Japanese order who are deathly afraid of the disease, is closed to all except Staff Officers and doctors. The question was immediately raised as to why they were in the area although our morale program covered the recital. The result; no music but two per week by the band. All instruments had to be turned in, not in the hands of the band, no singing by individuals or groups, ½ hour per day was allowed the band to practice, [same mass punishment]. This order has been somewhat liberalized today. We have received some medicines, 22,000 amoebacides, some aspirin, Nicotinious acid, and some odds and ends. The Japanese doctor ordered that only ameobic patients who would recover quickly should be treated. Our chief surgeon, of course, practically refused. It would have resulted in the active cases in the hospital receiving no treatment. One of the numbers played on our program last Wednesday, and very well done, was "The Breeze and I", Barbara's favorite. Took me back to the many happy hours we spent in their sitting room. May there be many more, my dearest.

January 22

No entries for a long time. The days go by interrupted only by small incidents concerning the administration of the camp. We still have received no mail for reasons best known to our hosts. The weather is quite unusual for this time of year as we are still having some rain. Our nights are cool, but days hot. We received another Red Cross box which will carry us until the end of February with care. Manila railroad reported out south of Manila. We believe shortage of equipment, as a train, seen by one of our work details in Cabanatuan, of five cars was pulled by three engines. Commissary by dint of getting permits fit from Japanese was able to send one of our vendors to Cagayan Valley. He brought back beans, 55 sacks at P150,000, 4000 eggs at P.40, some chickens at P10.50, a few ducks in a few cabbages[present]. We were given one of the first I have tasted since I've been on the island. Beatings have started on the farm again. This time, an officer, Captain Werment. Colonel Beecher protested, he believes, with some success. My health continues good. A cup of coffee in Manila said to be a P1.25 per, signs of inflation. I've just completed checking 4089 questionnaires as to the POWs present feelings; most harrowing experience, report of equipment failures, outbreak of disease, etc., to be like a propaganda, I guess. Deleted those which would anger them for no purpose.

January 29

Things go on without much change. The rains continue which is a blessing, for without our little gardens and the camp farm we would be absolutely without vegetables. As it is, except for a few bananas which the Americans bought, there has been no fruit of any type in our diet for at least three months. No meat, except the Red Cross boxes since late November, dried fish being issued in lieu thereof. Except for what is grown in individual gardens, we get a native white sweet potato called camote, its tops being supplied as greens. Sugar is nearly unattainable at any price. I bought a canteen cup on the black market; probably sold over the fence by the Japs for P10.00. The currency is nearly worthless. I saw a Manila Paper: among the For Sale items was a second-hand beauty parlor outfit; P10,000, Calesa pony with harness; P13,000, house and lot; P550,000. There arrived from Manila yesterday five sacks of mail from the U.S.A., approximately 25,000 letters. They, as far as I can find out, uncensored. 28 were delivered to us today, at this rate it will take 800 days. We were told there was more to come. We are required by the Japanese to be in bed by 9:00 PM, the reason unknown.

The Colonel's Way

January 31

Pay day. Also we were notified that beginning February 1, the rice ration would be cut 400 g with 250 g additional cut for worries of certain classes. The catch in it is that there is provided the substitution of corn or camote as the basic ration, as heretofore these items have been issued as a vegetable component. The net result will be, as rice is very short, that we will get camote or corn which we usually got as vegetables and grains, other components remain the same. Lieutenant Colonel Warner, a reserve officer from Baltimore who received one of the few letters distributed so far, showed me where someone had made an inquiry about me in the letter. I am not without some recognition at home. Nice feeling. Joe Ganahl got seven letters, five from Connie and two from his mother. Mine will be coming along soon I am sure. What happiness to look forward to.

February 5

One senior Medical Officer and his Adjunct were sent to Manila a few days ago and have returned. The purpose of the trip is not clear, even to them, they did nothing but talk to the senior Japanese doctor for a short while. They brought back some interesting items of interest. The train trip took 18 hours. They, with their guards, rode in a truck in or on a flatcar. Their reports of conditions is very dark. The natives are have starved and in rags. Rice is rationed at 240 g, but only 120g is issued by the control in agency when cards are presented, if there is any issue, which is seldom. The conditions are reported at various air fields where our men are working are beyond description, especially Nichols and Nielsen. Long hours, no decent food and many beatings. Mail is still in Manila for us. It seems that the mail now in camp, which is being delivered us about 75 letters per day, was all mailed to us prior to June 1943 and arrived here via Japan. That in Manila it arrived on the exchange ship which brought our Red Cross packages last fall and was mailed in the U.S. from June to September 15 when the boat sailed. There are also individual packages. If the system of censorship is not changed it will take years to get it. Our rice ration is way down in Mess #1, Group #1 on February 4. They were issued seven sacks of rice and ½ sacks of rice flour,[from our savings]. The strength for rations is 1050, each sack contains 50 kilos, if 350 g per man per day, not including rice flour.

February 8

Today was Lt. Col. Charles Leinbach's [F.A., U.S.A.] birthday. He is on Camp Staff and lives in our barracks. We had a fine party for him; roast duck and chicken [we couldn't get enough ducks], candied potatoes, fried bananas, coffee and a fine cake. We used our past prunes from Red Cross boxes in it. Everyone found a present of some kind for him. For once, we had enough to eat. Another detail; this time 150 Medical Corps and 50 doctors. We are at a loss to figure where they are to go. They are organized into four groups. Our efforts to get meat to the camp to be sold to the Japanese are showing results although none has actually come in. All plans are going well.

February 13

Sunday. Again I have let my wood cutting interfere with my going to church. It was unintentional as I planned to go but the time slipped by and it was after 11:00 AM when I got to take my bath. We received our last Red Cross food, one can powdered milk, four cans [large] of corn beef or spam, four cans butter, one can jam, one can ham and eggs, one canned corned pork, two packages of bouillon and soup. By fooling, we will make ours last until April at least. An additional detail of 300, including seven officers, has been called for. First called, a temporary detail, we expected to be used here on the islands, but later developments lead us to believe it may be going elsewhere. We examined all available well men and were only able to make available 36% to choose from. We are very short of well men. In addition, we have been called upon to furnish 500 men to work on the airport about 2.5 miles from camp. This combined with 500 for the farm takes all available well men and about 150 quarters to meet the quota. The Japanese have, for some reason, prohibited the use of amoebics on the wood cutting detail [outside] which is now composed entirely of officers [100]. Major Christiansen, who as a captain, was with me in the south, is to command the 300 men detail. He is a fine officer. I will miss him around camp. Mail continued to come over in small lots of 50 to 75 per day. So far, I've not been lucky. Valentine's Day tomorrow. I pray I may be with you by this time next year.

February 15

Rain today. Very unusual for this time of year. We are fortunate, for it will help the farm. Colonel Brady, 31st infantry, who is in charge of the 500 men at work on the airport asked me if something could be done to get the men working there more food as the lunch was so light that the men were faint from lack of food doing so much hard work. I made a survey of the rice rationed for today.

Group#1	Kitchen #1	#2	Group#2
Breakfast	70.8	70.6	71.6
Lunch	148.3	120.4	153.9
Dinner	120.4	148.3	379.4
Average	338.1	339.1	379.4

Average for camper rations 352.56. Rice substitute is issued: camotes 50 g. per ration and 50 g per heavy work POW. The heavy workers are supposed to get 200 g of extra rice. It is not issued. 50 g of salted fish per ration is issued and 25 g per heavy work. There is so much that is spoiled or full of maggots that we cannot eat that we average less than 50 g per ration. Vegetables, 300 g per ration, consist of camote tops or radishes with tops. The radish is large but contains mostly water and cellulose. I've yet to hit it lucky on the mail. Joe Ganahl got two letters from his Joe, age 12. He read them to me. So like our Sandy.

February 17

Major T.B. Maury,[F.A., Asst. Camp Adjunct], at one time C.O.; Group #1, was 34 today. Bill Shreve's age nearly to the day. We had a big feed, chop suey, boiled beans, and cake. My last box of prunes went in the cake. Spam from our Red Cross boxes made up the meat and our Sgt. Mitchel made wonderful noodles with rice flour and duck eggs. Maury received a little present from each of us. The Japanese who went to Batangas with are Filipino vendor to purchase bananas has not returned. Needless to say; no bananas.

February 20

Our vendor returned with only one truck load of bananas due to railroad break down. They arrived the day after market day and could only purchase what they could and locally. As the Japanese added the expenses of the guards, interpreter, etc., to the price of the lot, our price was up, 8.5 centavos per each banana. We had a set-back in our attempt to procure meat for this camp. Our scheme was, briefly, to arrange for some carabao vendor to purchase on the island [for any price] carabao and to sell them to the Japanese here at their controlled price, 20 centavos per kilo on the hoof. The difference plus reasonable profit to be paid by some group of loyal Filipinos, the necessary guarantee of payment be made by myself and some other officers, the involved were quite large, about 1 ½ times the cost of 'Our Decision'. The obligation was to be first on the U.S. government, if they failed to pay, it would be ours. Our agent reported today that a large group of Spanish Philippine citizens with whom we were evidently dealing, all names are in code, had been picked up by the Japanese M.P., cutting off our source of capital. We will have to try some other scheme. They are getting 150 to 200 pesos in Manila on the black market.

February 22

My first letters; words cannot describe my happiness! Yours of February 17 and March 12, 1943. Dearest, you, not I, are the brave and it is you whom I am so proud. I was distressed to hear of Bill Waxter's death. I will, of course, learn more when I get your #1,2,3,4,5 and #7 letters. Our boys! Oh dearest, you are so fine, they will be fine men, my Judy, because if you. We are so alike, Judy mine, our sleepless nights and our lives only half- lived when we are separated. I have faith, my Judy, that the day of our reunion is not so far away. I am, of course, curious about your move. I suspect servant and fuel trouble. I was overjoyed to hear of my mother. What of yours and Jay? But all will be cleared with more letters. I'm glad for mothers sake that Bill S. is near. Proud of our Sandy. All the camp knows the Colonel's son is head of the Junior Red Cross. I am sure you know where I am and that I'm okay by now. Our Decision must be lovely with what you've done. You were so smart to sell the sod to Brossine. I read your letters over and over, first thing in the morning, last thing at night.

February 25

The 300 officers and men; Medical detail, is to leave at 3:00 PM, 26th. They are outside our headquarters now receiving first aid kits, postal savings chits and last minute instructions. I am to be allowed to write you a letter but only about the receipt of Red Cross supplies. I cannot even say I am well. It is not hard to see through this one. In hopes of getting any word to our loved ones, we write only things favorable to the Japanese. Not me. As much as I want to communicate with you I cannot sell my birthright; letter attached. Gordon Schneider, civilian on duty at Camp #3 near here, came in on the ration truck. He reported that each Japanese soldier [139 or 140] connected with the Supply Corps there was issued by the Japanese 2 pound cans of Hershey cocoa which arrived in fresh new cartons. I suspect looting of Red Cross.

```
[attached letter, dated February 20, 1944]
Mrs. Arthur L.  Shreve
Tuscany apartments: E-3
Stony Run lane
Baltimore, Maryland


My darling Judy:
          The  Japanese  Military  authorities  have
allowed  me  through  you  to  communicate  to  the
International  Red  Cross  concerning  the  food  and
other  supplies  sent  to  the  American  prisoners  of
war.  On  Sunday,  November  28,  supplies  were
brought  to  this  camp,  the  first  since  November  of
last year,  under  the  supervision  of  the  Japanese
Military  Police.  Members  of  the  Military  Police
of  the  Japanese  Army  accompanied  the  Red  Cross
supplies  on  the  train  from  Manila.   They  were
delivered  to  us  in  trucks  guarded  by  members  of
the  Military  Police  Force,  to  whom  a  receipt  was
given  for  the  supplies  on  each  individual  truck.
Each  prisoner  of  war  received  a  little  more  than
four   individual   food   packages   -   two   invalid
```

packages, two regular packages. Any surplus was equally divided among all of the prisoners.

There were in addition about 600 cases of miscellaneous supplies, principally shoes, which were very acceptable as there was much need for them. There were also shoe repair kits, toilet articles, including laundry soap and toilet paper, cigarettes, tobacco, pipes, and recreational supplies. The Japanese authorities requested that they be given certain of the supplies to which we graciously acceded. Recently medicine has been received to fill our most urgent needs. Amoebacides and vitamin tablets were sorely needed and were received in large quantities. Cigarettes whose outer wrapper contained a patriotic verse were removed from the packages by the Japanese Military Police. The outer wrapper was removed and the[line out]National Red Cross authorities, especially the local Elementary Junior Representatives, the deep appreciation of every man here the bountiful supplies which have been sent to us. They have not only been a great source of enjoyment and health building food, but also tremendous factor in maintaining the morale of the prisoners of war.

Your devoted husband, Arthur L. Shreve
Lieutenant-Colonel
General Staff Corps
U.S. Army
Certified a true copy:
T.B. Maury III, Major, F.A.

February 29

Hot, dry weather. We have a 300 man detail still standing by, no date set for its departure. I read a note from an officer interned in Bilibid prison. He has been sorting mail and individual packages destined for American POWs. He said that there were 100,000 letters and thousands of packages. The letters uncensored, a part of which are destined for this camp, at the present rate, figuring our percent due and the rate at which the local Japanese authorities censor and deliver, it will take from 5 ½ to 6 years to get this mail. Of about 25,000 received here about February 1, we have received 1,650 in 32 days. I spend my days chopping wood, performing my few duties in trying to keep healthy. Nights are bad, I sleep so badly. I dream of you, my Judy, and the wonderful days when we are united again.

March 2

The Lord is good. It rained today for about ½ hour. Helps the farm and garden plots. The 300 man detail is being outfitted with clothing. Our naval uniforms for the men and the Japanese uniforms [too small] for the Officers. They are a strange sight with P. A. helmets. Again, we're having trouble on the farm. Beatings for no reason. We protest but get nowhere. Some hope for mail before the war is over. Four Japanese soldiers who can read American have come to help censor the mail. We have yet to receive any so cannot tell if the rate will increase. News is good. Colonel Beecher and I are making plans just in case we are still here when things change.

March 5

Darling, I'm so happy even if I am in prison camp. I've received two more wonderful letters from you, # 10 and # 11. You are such a wonderful girl to have gone through all you have not knowing if I were dead are alive and to carry on as you have. My eyes fill with tears of pride and love every time I read your letters. The first ones I received are nearly worn out. You are doing wonders with Our Decision, I know. I'm so glad you've had the lane fixed. Smart girl to make Cook pay half. I am relieved to hear that mother is well. So sorry about the Uncle Jim. Dearest, I too am sure that I will someday, not too far off, return to hold you in my arms again. Three hundred and eighty-six mail sacks with Parcels Post for us arrive on the 4th. After some maneuvering we finally got them stored on our side of the fence until a decision can be gotten from the Japanese as to their disposition and if they have to be searched for contraband. I hope not. Yours to me is in there, the names of recipients are on the tags on the sacks. Mashed my finger cutting wood. It does not help the printing.

March 9

Lt. Col. Johnson, our camp commissary and purchasing officer, returned from Manila. He went with a Japanese Supply sergeant to see the tobacco manufacturer in hope of getting more tobacco for us. He could do no good. The Japanese Military has taken over everything and no one knew anything or who to ask. But we received more mail yesterday, about 85. This makes 1,862 since January 29th, about 46 ½ per day, 2500 in all, figure it out; how long? 60 sacks of packages also arrived, this in addition to the 386, none have been released yet. After being on a dried fish ration since last fall, the Japanese told us that the fish had run out and they expected no more. Six head of carabao were brought in on the 8th and 16th. Today our issue of dressed meat was about 75 g per man, including bone. I must go to the dentist, he is cleaning and treating my gums. Wonderful to have them to keep our teeth in condition.

March 10

Japanese Army Day, we have a holiday. Cut wood this AM. We had a movie last night, first Japanese newsreel then "The Boys from Syracuse". The film was in terrible shape, kept breaking in the soundtrack was very bad, but we all enjoyed it. Anything that is a bit of home. Two small melons like watermelons P5.75 worth about 8¢ American money. Banana P.08, were 1¢. Beautiful moon these nights. I sit after all have gone to bed and dream of you and moonlit nights when I was with you, Hawaii, Ohio, Sill, Indiana, Ocean City, all were so perfect they will come again. News is good.

March 12

Cool, very unusual for this time of year. Last night around 8:00 PM, Lt. Col. Johnson, our Commissary officer, brought me a paper to sign as President of Camp Council. It was to the effect that he and I, as authorized representatives of the Camp Council, did release the Imperial Japanese Army for responsibility of the P15,000.00 entrusted to them to purchase cigarettes fit from 'Primco' was lost through brigand or highway robbery. They said that they would, "Fight to the death to protect your money, but things are very bad so we must have a release." Such are conditions here. Must go to supper. Pfc. Bell, [colored] died in the hospital. He had been retired long ago and had come back in. He was in his late sixties.

March 14

Still no package distribution. We received 125 letters yesterday. The supply has been notified that we will receive two carabao per week as a meat ration. This will seriously affect our health. In a few months we will be back to where we were in September and October, 1942. High death rate and sickness. Our agent with 27 sacks of beans and 20 sacks of peanuts was intercepted by the Japanese from Manila and his supplies were requisitioned. He was paid the control price, about half of the cost to him and no transportation. He must have lost about P6000 to P7000.

The loss of the beans to us is beyond description. I have a slight cold but still continue my exercise. If the food is to continue so poor, I will have to cut down on the wood cutting or I will lose weight which I cannot afford.

March 16

At 6:30 PM after waiting without supper for 1 hour, the most exciting officer in this camp, I am sure, was given a package from the most wonderful girl in all the world. The tooth powder could not stand the strain of the trip, but after a little dusting off, prove to be okay. My dear, if I had picked the things myself they could not have been better. "The pipe" is most acceptable as I only had one, and after two years of continuous smoking, it is a bit strong. You have a wonderful memory, my favorite candy, the almonds and the Nestles cocoa you knew I loved. 67 letters yesterday, still slow. It gets hotter and dustier each day. No meat since Monday.

March 17

Smoking of my new pipe and thinking of my love who sent it to me. The General in charge of prison camp, [a new one, General Morimoto, late incumbent, having been relieved and gone to Japan according to Japanese officers here], inspected today. No report as to his views or a policy. No mail, no packages. I inspected a mess.

Our ration of rice is about 350 gr. of rice per day of which about 50 is ground for rice cake, etc. which leaves about 100 gr. per meal. Supper consisted of baked camote, rice cake, [our purchased sugar to supplement issue], camote soup, tea, pickled greens. No meat or substitute since March 13. The other mess; same rice, same soup, boiled greens, coconut [our purchase] cornstarch pudding, tea. We were most fortunate: you're prunes produced a pie, omelet with corned beef [Red Cross] then as above [the second]. I was cutting wood right beside the fence when the General was scheduled, in grand stand seat, but the Japs made us stop. I will admit the costume was not fetching. G-string, shoes and socks.

March 19

Finish my chopping and attended in my new socks and belt with a new handkerchief in pocket. I went to communion in the PM. I put a new handle in my axe. The Japs called for a 200 man local detail. Check shows 346 well men in camp, this including all S. D. on our side and Jap side. We're getting very low. The hot season is here, food is poor and scarce. Two more days and all packages will be distributed.

March 24

Lt. Commander Jordon, U.S.N., Japanese language officer who acts as one of two interpreters on the camp farm, was beaten and kicked down by a Jap soldier from headquarters who counts the men in and out of the gate. I've investigated the incident and all available witnesses. I find no justification. Colonel Beecher will protest. This occurred at about 5:00 PM today.

March 26

Lucky me, I received another from my sweetheart and one from mother last evening, your #9 nine, April 1, 1943. Dancing class for our boys? It seems incredible that they are that big. You are doing all the things I knew you would do. I am so proud. Good for Ned Searby. He is a good man, will make a good B. C. Mothers letter was quite cheerful. So glad Bill S. is fortunate to be near home. You spoke of the young apple trees. You must have put those in. I finish studying a book on farm management. There's a lot to learn. You, I'm sure by your letters, will be an expert on rock gardens when I get back. Our weekly issue of meat averaged 123.5 g per man or about 17 gr. per day per man.

Friday, March 31

Twenty-five percent of 1944 has passed. If all goes as well as the first part, this war will be over before 1945. Monday at 11:30 AM as I was returning from my bath, I saw a Jap soldier beating four of our men on their bare backs with a stick. They were carrying a large litter of camotes; reason for punishment I could not ascertain. We received 92 kilos of meat today for 1,915 men. About 50 g of bone and meat per man, last issue as above. I read your letters over and over, my Judy. It helps so to have them, though it does not help the sleeping. Too many days of dreams. I live over our happy years, our trips together. There were no unhappy moments. While I cut wood or work in the garden, I find myself smiling at some incident over our wonderful life together. It is hot these days. I feel for the men on the airport and the farm. The Japs will require some of our men to go without shoes on the farm. We're trying to get permission for them to wear shoes.

April 1

Through our efforts based on the heat and short rations, the Japanese have changed the work hours, now 7:00 AM to 11:00 AM and 3:00 to 4:30 PM, except on the airport where our men leave at 8:00 AM and return at 4:30 PM. A letter from the U.S. Treasury to Private Harvey Michaels, notifying him that his sister had purchased some bonds in his favor, was withheld by the Japs. One of our adjuncts saw the notice in the Jap headquarters and tried to get it released, in this way he was able to notify Michaels. This is but one of many instances of mail being withheld. I have arranged for salt to be issued to the men to be taken when working in this heat. Our source of news is gone.

April 3

American Medical headquarters told me today that the Jap doctor said our weekly issue of meat was to be increased to 10 g. per man per day, 70 g. per week. The following is interesting:

RATION SUMMARY
Average per day per man

Month	Protein Gr.	Fat Gr.	Carbohydrate Gr.	Calories
3-43	73.00	44.91	555.00	2930.00
4-43	70.45	42.37	528.6	2748.00
5-43	64.08	44.04	519.7	2747.00
6-43	62.29	40.89	502.2	2622.00
7-43	57.41	40.96	484.83	2534.00
8-43	58.85	44.68	434.46	2362.1
9-43	67.49	41.56	461.77	2488.23
10-43	63.3	43.32	477.42	2552.1
11-43	57.9	40.26	510.21	2624.6
12-43	55.75	33.18	411.12	2485.2
1-44	68.01	25.52	455.72	2360.6
2-44	60.33	30.53	375.99	2010.9
3-44	40.04	27.79	344.16	1786.6

The Colonel's Way

April 4

After nearly two years a faint light begins to show through the darkness. Our hope that someday our forces would arrive before we were all sent to Japan looks as though it may come true. Japanese headquarters has told us that about 4000 American POWs, just about the number now away from this camp on temporary details, are to be returned soon, 60 to 90 days or less. With what news we have, two and two adds up; they expect an attack. Oh dearest- it may be that our long separation may be coming to an end and that in less than three years total, I will be with you. Three years; 1000 lonely days and nights when I am only half alive for without you, I am only that.

April 7

Good Friday, and second in prison. Yesterday we wrote a letter to the camp Commanding Officer suggesting that mail deliveries could be increased. Maceda, one of the interpreters, took offense. We offered to withdrawal the letter but were refused. He has taken it upon himself to discipline us. No mail for two days. Hot and dry.

April 9, Easter Sunday

I went to communion after cutting wood with Joe Ganahl. The Japs released 295 letters, first in three days. I'm sure that we will not be prisoners next Easter. I expect and plan to go to church with you, my love, next Easter.

April 14

Yesterday I inspected the medical records in this camp. I find that the hospital records are in good shape, the infirmary records not so. Books on one and cards on another, no records being transferred with men from group to group, no office of record for non-active files. I took the question up with Colonel Beecher this morning and with Medical Headquarters. They were not too receptive but promised to get a consolidation and filing of non-active records in Medical Headquarters. I'm very restless and have a terrible time sleeping. I dream of you constantly. I know I'll be all right when I can be near to you, my Judy. I love you so.

April 17

The days slip by, hot and dusty. We had light rain yesterday which helped to cool the air and we had a nice cool night. The ration has been out again, 300 g rice, 100 g corn. The camotes will be furnished; 350 g per working man as long as they last. I may not have mentioned this before, but ever since the farm has been producing, the choice vegetables have been taken by the Japs; both for Camp #3 and here. The statement that everything produced on the farm would be placed to our credit to buy meat with, has [of course] never been lived up to. We now get two issues of two animals per week, about 130-150 g of carcass per man, or 4 to 5 ounces of meat and bone. The following figures are interesting:

Commissary prices	Oct. 1943	April 1944
P=pesos		
Camotes – kilos	P .35	P.60
Hens eggs – each	P.20	P.60

Duck eggs – each	P.27	P.77
Salted peanuts, ganta	P 3.20	P5.50
Mongo beans, ganta	P.3.20	P12.50
Bananas – kilo	P.50	P 1.25
Black beans	P 3.60	P13.00
Coconuts-each	P.15	P.35
Sugar(63)Kilo sack	P16.20	P33.50
Cigarettes[Phil] Pkg.	P.22	P.45
Peanuts [raw sugar cake]-kilo	P1.95	P5.50

Jap controlled prices through "PRIMCO".

April 23

Sunday. I did not go to church, had a shot for Cholera this AM. Japanese origin, our Medical officers doubt its worth. We had our first good rain this PM, the first this dry season. We are averaging about 100 letters per day, much better. The Japs have stopped the beatings on the farm and have lately turned all culprits to us for punishment. I hope we can break up the stealing of vegetables. It is hard. The men are so hungry. What little news we get is good. I feel we will not be here six months from now. We have new books and the library. I study all I can find on farming. It makes me feel close to you as I know you spend a lot of time at our place.

April 25

Oh my dearest, you never miss a chance to send me words of cheer and love and it makes me very happy. Today when I returned from cutting wood there was a telegram from you dated April 1, Tokyo, so recent. I know you knew in December that I was okay. My faith has never faltered, we will be united again in the not too distant future. We are in the height of the hot season and for the first time in months I am without sugar with no hopes of getting any.

April 28

Up at 2:00 AM to meet 150 patients and five others from Bilibid. The men look very badly, thin and pale, dressed in rags. None of them will ever recover from this ordeal; most of them with Beri Beri with optical neuritis, slowly going blind. Another scorcher. Even the Japs suffer. The sun is north of us now, being directly overhead a few days ago. To get in the shade, you sit on the south side.

May 2

Captain Blackledge was beaten on the farm today. I investigated and had Colonel Engelhart, the chief interpreter and American in charge on the farm, investigate also. A case of language difficulty, but entirely uncalled for. The serious part was that the Japs would not allow Blackledge to receive first aid. He had a bad scalp wound. A.P. headquarters has protested in writing.

May 3

The bull cart drivers were taken to the Jap guard, no use after the carts came in and were unloaded. The first I knew of it, Colonel Johnson [commissary] came to me to hide some of his papers. Mr. Threatt, a civilian in charge of the drivers, as he approached the unloading platform inside the fence managed, though closely watched, to whisper to Colonel Johnson; "The fat is in the fire."

The Colonel's Way

The drivers had been one of our main contacts with the outside, partially by collusion with the guards and partially by the use of a canteen with a false bottom. Mrs. Threatt, acting as a waitress in a small shop, fills Mr. Threatt's canteen with water for him, taking it from view to do so. Upon its return to him and also when he is searched at the gate, he drinks from it and puts a little water on his hands and face to allay suspicion. Threatt and his men must have known that something was up. Not only his words to Colonel Johnson, but while in unloading the carts, they unloaded too, dropping the canteen, belt and shoulder bags which were picked up and disappeared. One of the drivers dropped as sawali bag in a dry ditch on the road outside the fence near the Power Station. Major Reynolds sent a man who works over on that side to retrieve it while he and I watched the Japs. Threatt and his men were taken away and searched. Nothing but some money and razor blades were found; all are being detained incommunicado. We are all very anxious. Some money had been secured by notes signed by U.S. [see February 20 – 44] and had been cashed 7.5 to one. That money has been left outside. Commodities purchased and delivered [Japs do not check weights] are deducted from this fund. Our invoices and receipts via bull cart drivers. Some had left this morning.

May 5

Our men are still being held by the Japs. As far as we can determine, they are well- treated. We feed them, send them cigarettes and coffee. Our minds are much relieved. Lieutenant Itoh [Jap] has, contrary to Japanese orders, been purchasing American cigarettes from prisoners of war, and as we in Camp Headquarters had procured some for him [P5.00 ea.], we sort of have them on the hip. Major Maury asked him what the men were being held for. He told us that the Jap M. P. in Cabanatuan had raided a shop or shops and had found notes and money addressed to persons in camp, but as far as he knew, there was nothing to connect our drivers and nothing had been found on them. The Jap M.P.s are having our men held, not Camp Headquarters. Hot, dry weather. I weigh 149 or 50. Not bad.

May 11

Evil days are upon us. Yesterday in addition to Threatt and his five men, the Jap M.P.s descended upon camp and took our first nine and then two more. The unfortunate part is that one of our men undoubtedly, when put under pressure, squealed; as I have the word of Lt. Col. Montgomery McKee, U.S.A. and Maj. Wade Cothran, F.A., Res., that they heard and saw Pt. H.K. Ballew, F.A., identify P. D. Rogers [Ex. Gov. of Jolo] to the Japanese as the man to whom he gave a note. Subsequently, Lt. Colonel Mack was picked up. List of those taken are the following:

Bull Cart Drivers:

Bish, Seth C.	S/Sgt., MD	Group 1
Burns, Virgil P.	S/Sgt., VC	" 1
Phillips, Breed S.	Pvt.	" 1
Tysinger, Raymond L.	ACMM, USN	Grp. 11
Ross, Robert A.	Sgt., USME	Grp. 11
Threatt, Fred G.	Civilian	" 1

Other:

*Mack, Edward G.	Lt. Col.	Group 1
Baldwin, Lee	Capt.	" 1

Byrne, Patrick J.	Capt.		1
Le Mire, Jack F.	Capt.	Group	1
Sherk, Robert H.	1st Lt.	Gr.	11
Patrick, Darvin O.	T/Sgt., MD	Hosp.	
Ballew, Herbert K.	Pvt.	Gr.	11
Tyler, Floyd E.	1st Sgt.	Gr.	1
Churakovsky, Vladimir B.	Civ.	Gr.	1
Jasten, Walter	Civ.	Group	1
*Rogers, Paul D.	Civ.	Gr.	1

*Not taken in the first round-up.

But these men were evidently questioned all yesterday afternoon and some last night and this morning in company with some Filipinos, one who has been working for one of our vendors, and one of the vendors, were all loaded on a truck and taken out of camp, destination and fate of unknown. The truck stopped at the gate where more Filipinos were loaded and then proceeded west. Yesterday I checked the Group and Hospital Commissaries to assure myself that their books would stand inspection. I also disposed of Main Commissary surplus funds and papers. During disposition the Japs went into the building next door. Close-but we made it. I wrote a card to you yesterday. We are to be allowed to date them this time. There is so little I can say of what I would like to. If the Japs object to what you say, they simply tear up the card. You have no chance to correct it.

May 12

Quite some time has passed and no search, so have dug out my book again today. I went to the hospital to have some calcium deposits removed from under my left eye,[Major Wilson; EEM &T].Just afterwards while talking to Colonel Schwartz ,our chief surgeon, he was sent for by A.P. headquarters. I walked up with him to find there Colonel Oliver, Chief Chaplain; Captain Aton, V.C.; Captains [Chap] Zimmerman and Taylor. They were sent to Jap headquarters where they were taken by the M.P. in a truck to, we believe, Cabanatuan. This is borne out by the Japs order to our Camp Supply officer, Col. Britell, to furnish rations for 17 men. These were then placed on a truck and taken to Japanese headquarters in Cabanatuan by one of our truck drivers. This was on May 12. On May 13, Lt. Bob Sherk was returned to this camp, but held in Jap guard house. Lt. Jack Sherk and Captain [Chap] Tiffany were arrested and taken out on May 15. Pvt. Ballew was returned to Jap guard house. On May 16, Bish, Burns, Phillips, Tysinger, Ross and Jasten were returned to Jap guardhouse. Late this PM, Capt. [Chap] Zimmerman was also returned.

May 19

No further development in the investigation. There are two men in camp who were called but not taken out. From them we find that the course of the investigation points to a search for the outside source of notes. Money, so far, has not been mentioned at least during the questioning of these two.

May 20

Two wonderful letters from you, Judy mine. I was so proud of you. Your courage is magnificent to go on as you do and have done all only on hope; no words, no news, to help you. Never a word of complaint or a note of despair, your letters are cheerful and encouraging. I am glad you had a phone put in. The minute I get out of here, I'm going to call you. Now, even if you are at Our Decision, I can reach you. Interesting figure is on average waits

The Colonel's Way

taken at the end of the period, April 16, 2 May 14, showing loss by groups and were categories: group #1--7 lbs., group # 2-2 lbs., hospital –[4 months ending is above] 6.3 lbs., heavy workers – 3.65 lbs., non- workers – 5.15 lbs., [non-workers including Quarters and per Qtrs., all fatigue and kitchen details inside the fence, and all senior officers, clerks, etc.] Captain Chunn was called, interviewed and returned, same line of questioning. I love the snap of the view from Our Decision. You and the boys could have been a little more in evidence. I am deep in a book on chicken raising written by the head of the poultry department, University of Maryland; Junn by name. Very good.

May 21

While I was in the hospital visiting today, the Jap M.P. truck came in with the remainder of the men and officers held. They were taken to the other side and, of course, we do not know their eventual disposition. We are to no end pleased to see them come in for we believe it will be only a matter of time before they will be returned to our side. Returned were Threatt, Mack, Baldwin, Byrne, LeMire, Sherk [Jack], Patrick, Tyler, Churakovsky, Rogers, Oliver, Schwartz, Aton, Taylor, Tiffany. Everyone in camp feels much better as to the eventual outcome. Food is scarce. Everyone complains of being hungry all the time. We received, on Friday last, a small donation from the Neutral Aid community in Manila. Tomatoes, onions, beans, jam, about 16 kilos of meat, soy sauce, cigars and cigarettes [one each]. We had a good soup for one meal. I have lost only 5 pounds since January. I am, fortunately, an easy keeper.

May 22

Word has just come to me of the death of my mother. It is of course a shock. As much as one steels oneself knowing that our dear ones are old and that their days with us are numbered, when the time arrives, it makes it no less hard to bear. Words cannot express my admiration and love for her. All that I have done or made of myself in this world I owe largely to two people; you and her. I hoped to see her again, but I guess she was not sorry. Father died 31 years ago, a long time for a woman to be alone. I have yet to receive the word from the Japs. It was sent to me by our Ex. A.P. Hq. Sgt. Major who saw it in Bilibid. I wonder how long it will take for them to get it from Manila, 125 kms. My friends have been very kind. The war has taken its toll on our family. Please God, there will be no more. I know so well that you are splendid and that you and our boys were a great joy to her. She never failed to praise you in her letters.

May 23

The General was to inspect today but he spent his time going through our own hospital area, kept us standing around for 3 hours waiting and never showed up. Thirteen of those arrested and held by M.P.'s were released to us today. They were told not to talk on threat of being arrested again. Capt. Byrne, Capt. Zimmerman, Lts. Sherk,[Jack and Bob]; Sgts. Burns, Bish, and Patrick; Pvt. Phillips; CMM Tysinger, Sgt. Ross; 1st. Sgt. Tyler; Civ. Jasten and Churakovsky. As to the others, we have no word. We are doing all we can or are allowed to do for them.

May 25

Lucky me. I got another letter from my love last night, your #4, written February 1, 1943. The Plim sale was made which I did not know, also about Waxter. I'm overjoyed that you have been able to get the allotment increased. I know you will manage well, and it is a help to know that you do not have any financial worries. Sorry about the tooth and Sandy's arm. The official copy of your wire arrived today enclosed. Food is very scarce. I know what it is to be hungry all of the time. But back to better things. I cannot figure how I could have all the service you claim, but I am glad you get more pay.

May 27

Captain [Chap] Tiffany, one of the number still held on the Japanese side, was returned to this side on a stretcher. He had been suffering from bacillary dysentery. He was having a chill at the time of his return. He had been ill for six days before he was allowed to have medical attention. This is typical. After more than a year I have given up cutting wood. Food is just too scarce. I am taking over the garden in hopes of getting more from that source. Lt. Col. Johnson, [Camp C.O.], was called to Jap headquarters, subject; new system of purchase and delivery of supplies. The Japs Supply officer is to act as agent in all but one case. He will buy through the Japanese Association. O'Fugi is to continue to come in. Colonel Johnson feels that O'Fugi [Jap Lt.] is sincere. For the tremendous price increase we will fare as well as before. No X. account will be possible as no money will get in for a long time.

The Colonel's Way

May 28

With the aid of some of my Bahai companions, I dug up another garden plot. We'll put in some sort of greens. Went to church, Communion with a memorial service as it was the nearest Sunday. The Chaplain said a lovely prayer in memory of mother. I asked him to, as I could not be at her funeral. I felt better about it as I feel that I had participated in a service for her. No word of our men and officers held by the Japs. The men are so hungry that we have to put guards on the individual gardens at night.

June 4

No entries for some time. Things go along. The Japanese made a partial issue of clothes; shorts[under] for about 75 or 80% and a so-called towel, one each. The towel; a piece of unbleached rough cotton cloth, 7 inches wide by about 20 inches long. Soap was also issued. Everyone is hungry. The men collect and cook weeds, potato skins, etc. It is hard to watch the so-called garbage from the kitchen being picked over by the men as it is being carried to the sumps. Old pieces of tin and any old cans serve as stew pots. The Jap lieutenant has told us that bananas are on the way. Tobacco is terribly scarce. I am smoking in my pipe [2] plain sun dried leaf which I cut up myself. Captain Jack LeMire was returned to us as Tiffany was; on a stretcher, bacillary dysentery, quite ill. He told us this much. When they [all] were returned from Cabanatuan, they were told by the M.P.s that they were through with them. Mr. Teto [interpreter] told them to sit down, that they would soon be sent to this side. Major Twanaka, Camp C.O., came out, sent those listed as returned to this side and the remaining [10] to the Jap guardhouse. They were first placed in a very small shack – so small that they could hardly lie down. The Jap general, on the day he inspected, evidently ordered them placed elsewhere, for they are now are under a shed [lean- to] beside the guardhouse. I weigh 140 lbs.

June 7

News, which comes to us in a miraculous manner, was good yesterday. Rome fell this morning came news of the invasion of Europe. Still no hope of more food. Our issue of rice, made by the sack, supposed to weigh 100 kilos, is invariably short. Yesterday in Group #1 alone [strength 1100 to 1200] they were 200 rations short and today 230. This, is on top of our short rations, is bad. Prices of things outside are terrific. Sugar cake, native product, must be boiled and cleaned before fit to use. P5.00 for two small cakes, P 16.50 a kilo. Manila cigarettes in Cabanatuan, according to the Japs, 30¢ each, or P9.00 a package. Colonel Johnson was offered some beans today by one of the vendors to the Japs for P16.00 a canteen cup.

June 10

Terribly hot weather. Our diet consists of boiled rice[gruel] another for breakfast, steamed rice with corn[1/3], sometimes a few greens and tea for lunch. Same for supper, plus a small cookie may with rice flour. We are temporarily out of sugar so we get no cookie these days. Our vegetable is varied; from greens to baked pumpkin. The men who work outside the fence for the Japs and on work details receive 300g extra either of corn or camotes. Twice a week we receive meat at the rate of 50 g per man per issue [meat and bone]. On this, one is hungry all the time and weight loss is terrific. I doubt if one will starve. A few eggs [65¢] and some green papaya is all that we have been able to get in. We have

The Colonel's Way

bought eggs with our money which is about exhausted now. I work hard trying to raise a few vegetables, but with the bugs, heat and poor ground, it is very discouraging. The value of the peso is dropping fast. We have made a plea to Jap headquarters to increase our pay. My weight seems to be holding at 140 pounds.

<u>June 13</u>

Captain Lee Baldwin, [C.of E.] was sent to the hospital from the Jap guardhouse [Sacroiliac Arthritis] yesterday. Colonel Johnson, much to our surprise, was allowed to go to Cabanatuan with the Jap Supply sergeant. He reports prices skyrocketing. Peanuts; P20.00 a ganta. He priced a hoe head: P18.00. Our success in Italy and France have had their effect. To our request for toilet paper, the Japs suggested that we make it. Our Supply officer thought they were joking, where upon they became very indignant. Food is the topic of conversation. It is very scarce, no sugar, no vegetables in the messes, rice and corn only, no tea today. We received, through the commissary, one kilo of panutsa [sugar cake] P12.50. You must be busy at Our Decision. I worry that you work too hard. You're never out of my thoughts.

<u>June 15</u>

253 officers and men from Bilibid. Hospital and quarters cases. 97 without blankets. Japs have, or will furnish, none. Lt. Col. 'Bob' Lindsay was among them. He looks well but thin. His cheerful good humor will be welcome. When their bags were searched, the local Japs had a fine looting party. All Red Cross cigarettes were taken, along with local brands of cigarettes and tobacco, which they will sell to our men at tremendous prices. I have been investigating the hospital mess for alleged leaks. It appears that

the accusations were unfounded. Food is so scarce in everyone so hungry that all sorts of charges are made. Sugar has been removed from the list of articles to be supplied prisoners of war by the Jap Army. The local Jap Supply officer has notified our S.O., but says he has money to buy it, or sugar substitute. I doubt if they can buy either. Very little, if anything, has come into our commissary. A few packages of cigarettes, some tobacco and a few eggs. Our hopes of the Japs being able to get things for us is fading. Our request for increase in pay received [40 pesos F.O.; 30 Company officers] is not favorably considered by Manila headquarters, we have been told. Our place must be lovely now. Oh dearest, to be there with you again. Rains are quite frequent, nearly daily now.

June 19

We have been in or near a typhoon for the past four days with hard rains. It has reduced the bug menace in the garden, but is added to the problem of the tropical garden. Everything has to be hilled or the rain washes the dirt away from the roots. Speaking of gardens and produce, with everyone here at the point of slow starvation, the Jap shipped out from the farm today nine [9] long tons of vegetables. We have been given an allowance, 200 g per day. I believe that the Japanese would let the vegetables on the farm rot rather than exceed it. 150 men detailed locally leaves tomorrow at 3:50 AM. I dreamed of you last night, my love. I was so alone when I awakened. I lay under my mosquito bar and heard the bell sound; 11:30, 12:00, 1:00, 1:30 AM before I fell asleep again. I still am confident of victory in this calendar year. We have struck at Japan proper [air] and are pressing her hard from the sea.

June 20

I will have to retract my statement of yesterday. The Japs today sent us in quite a lot of cucumbers there were about to spoil. Rains continue. I am having a reoccurrence of my old trouble [hemorrhoids]. Hope I can get well without being operated on. In the condition I am in, recovery would be slow and painful. Due to lack of fuel, our water pumps are inoperative from 2:00 PM until dark, about 7:30 PM. The night pumping is done from the upper well, a poor producer, by electricity. The lower well [diesel] is pumped from about 6:00 AM until 2:00 PM. Water is off from 12:00 PM to 5:00 PM. Johnson and I are plugging a scheme to pull all but a small portion of pay[P5.00] per individual receiving pay. This fund, to be a general mess fund. Those receiving pay would fare worse, but all would benefit. Its chance of success, I am afraid, is small. Distrust of those in authority, I am sorry to say.

June 23

Clear hot days. I am better but am to go to the hospital Monday night for a minor operation. I will not have to stay, but will have to stay close to my bed for a day or so. The Japs have increased our vegetable ration to 200 g. Cucumbers are all we get for supper. Our ration consisted of boiled rice with hominy with cucumber cooked in it and a piece of cucumber on the side. To this was added a fish-tasting gravy of ground rice and coconut oil. The fish taste was furnished by our welfare fund through the medium of a 5 gallon can of salt fish and shrimp at the modest price of P150.00; P5.00 a 5gal. can before the war.

The Colonel's Way

June 24

We had a meeting of representatives of the men and officers today. As I had predicted, we are not meeting with much success. Motives are too selfish. Everyone's plan is to get the other fellow to put up his money for the general good, or, if he contributes, to reserve for himself some privilege. We [Johnson and me] appointed a board to draw up a plan which will be submitted to the camp for approval or disapproval. That is all we can do. 400 men, 4 Line officers, 2 Medical officers, 6 Corps men [Med. Dep.] ordered out – looks like Japan. We will be pressed to carry on here. The airport will have to be cut. I think of you at Our Decision. Someday, dearest, I will live again when we are united. I love you so.

June 26

The surgeon will not operate, not at present at least. I am so much better. Quite a relief. Our vegetable ration still remains cucumbers and has been reduced 100 g that it was increased the other day. Our chief surgeons report to American prisoner headquarters for June 1 to 25, shows non-Japanese workers ration 1685.20 calories per day; authorized Jap workers additional 1008 calories. It is wonderful that our sick rate is no higher. It will come if our food, especially protein, is not increased. The Jap experience with their first issue of corn as a ration is too good not to record. First, they tried boiling it, as they do rice. It was, of course, hard and the husk was still on the grain. So, as they had heard that the Americans used ashes [lye] so they put the boiled corn on a table and sprinkled it with dry ashes. This, not appearing right, they decided to sprinkle it with water. In true oriental form, one of the cooks filled his mouth with water and blew it on the mixture and awaited

The Colonel's Way

results. Nothing happened, so they took to be beating it with clubs until it was, of course, ruined. They sent for two men, special duty, as cooks. Jap kitchen qualifications: must know how to fix corn.

June 27

Our detail leaves at 7:30 AM tomorrow. A detail of 70 arrive from Bilibid; 25 duty, 45 disabled. Another detail will arrive tomorrow, 69 officers, 642 enlisted. They are to be put in the old hospital area and kept incommunicado. We believe they are from Davao. There are ugly rumors about their trip up; two[2] were reputed as escaping in Zamboanga, from then on up,[20 days], they were kept in the holds; though one more managed to escape over the side. Upon arrival in Manila, over 40 had had to be carried off on stretchers, 200 were seriously ill. Our medical report, May 25 to June 25, shows group #1 and #2 strength: 3079; pellagra/ nutritional edema: 1043, over 25% affected. Weight loss average, group #1-2.4 pounds, group #2 -3.7 pounds, Hospital – 3.6 pounds, not a pretty picture. We continue to press Japan hard on the Pacific front with great success. If I can remain here, I believe, early fall will see the end. In my search for knowledge in agriculture, I find chemistry is lacking. So I have embarked on a course; my instructor, Lt. Col. Peoples, my classmate at Leavenworth.

June 30

Tomorrow will be our Douglas' birthday; also the first half of the year has slipped away -our last calendar year of the war. The Japs are either very sure of their position here or are they do not care if they lose us, for, from all appearances, this camp is quite

The Colonel's Way

permanent. They have shipped up from Davao or all sorts of junk trucks full of old, patched 5 gallon cans, an old one cylinder engine, and no end of just junk; too numerous to describe. The system of guarding has changed our sentries. The Japanese posts theirs <u>inside</u> the fence. Why? Not a word comes from our fellow prisoners in the old hospital area. We supply them and will pay and administer them, but we are not allowed to speak to them. No change in rations. We did get 15 g per man sugar issue on the 28th; first since June 8. Everyone is hungry. Several dogs have died of starvation the last two weeks. I have enough saved from my Red Cross enough to eat 1- 3 ½ ounce can of high protein food each week, which I am doing, to last until the first week in August. What then? We have hopes. There's no tobacco in camp. I will have to stop smoking tomorrow.

<u>July 1</u>

To our Douglas, many happy returns of the day. I know he's enjoying his 10th birthday, for, so well do I know his adorable mother, I know she will provide for him all that is heart desires. That memory I live again, that mad dash from Fort Knox to arrive too late. I will be there for his 11th. We issue ration for 684 total in the old hospital area; our first figure must have been an error. We are to reorganize the camp soon, by order of the Japs. Group #1 and #2 are to be equalized. All active Amoebics are to be sent to the hospital. As we know that this order came from Manila, it has no appearance of breaking up this camp. I work in the garden each day and soon, I believe, we will begin to harvest.

The Colonel's Way

July 2

A lovely day- sunshine, a breeze and no rain. We were paid today, and with the exception of a little work in the garden, I've taken it easy. One has to on this ration. Today, with nothing extra, we had rice gruel with the leftover broth from last night, a little flavor of meat was all one could detect. Lunch: steamed rice and corn with a spoonful of greens; supper: the same plus a rice cookie [sour from yeast with a little sugar in it]. Such is our daily bread.

July 5

We have had another reorganization. First, it was ordered that the groups be equalized, and then on the night of the 3rd, the Japs brought out another plan for the administration of the camp. A Prisoners of War Office is to be established with a Japanese officer at its head; under him, 10 American officers: Adjunct, Medical, Utilities, Library, Quartermaster, Finance: Officer Pay, Finance: Enlisted Pay, Commissary, Statistical, Work Details. Each division [old groups] including Hospital, to report directly to P. of W.D. It was evident that with no coordinator, the thing would not work. Colonel Beecher decided, after a talk with us, [staff] to recommend to the Japs a coordinator or executive. If this did not meet their approval, some senior officer would be recommended for one of the staff positions as listed above, and he, by mutual agreement of the Prisoners of War, would coordinate the command. On July 4, Colonel Beecher was sent for. During the interview, he convinced them of the coordinator solution. To give me some official status, he recommended me as Officer in charge of Salaried Pay, so I believe that the problem is solved. There are, of course, details to be worked out, but in the main, the system will work.

July 6

The Japanese, and very wisely I think, deleted the Office of Salaried Pay, so I am out of a job. Colonel Beecher kindly agreed to let me stay where I am so I do not have to move away from my garden.

July 8

Last evening there was quite a commotion on the Japanese side. All of the officers and NCOs were assembled and, as far as we could ascertain, were given a talk by a Field Officer who returned from Manila with Major Iwanaka, C.O., this AM. Being Imperial Rescript Day, all of the Japanese garrison, except those on duty, were paraded and the Rescript read to them. Afterward, much to our surprise, they were lined up along the road in one of their farewell formations. Two our further surprise, Major Iwanaka and Lt. Hirota left among "Banzai's." Soon thereafter, we were told to be prepared to be inspected by the new C.O., name not given. He duly arrived, late as usual, made a tour through camp and return to the Japs side to do the same. Later in the morning a Captain Scarda, 515 Cal. [AA], came to me to report that the new C.O. was Major Takaihashi and that he had been Military Governor of Bataan while Scarda to command of a detail there, from September to the end of December 1942. I took Scarda to Colonel Beecher and he described Takaihashi as certainly not anti-American, fond of women and wine, a good administrator who insisted that the POWs be well-fed and well-treated, well-cared for medically and that he understood and spoke American fairly well. We believe he has been sent here due to the change in policy, as to change policy without changing the C.O. would cause lots of 'loss of face'. Major Iwanaka sent a message that he was sorry not to have had a chance to give the staff and senior officers a good-bye talk, but he had not the time, as the change was unexpected. As to my position, Colonel Beecher told me he was going to recommend to the Japanese that I be appointed Morale Officer, which will keep me on duty at headquarters. Our former morale officer, Colonel Montgomery, has never been officially recognized by the Japs. Colonel Beecher's idea it is to allow him to continue heretofore. My position, I have yet to consult with him about.

July 9

Sunday, worked in the garden this AM. Just after lunch we received through the Japs for commissary 16- 20 kilo sacks of beans at P30.80 a ganta, 1085 packs of tobacco, 250 g each at P3.80. The Jap interpreter, as they are so careful about POWs leaving camp, had to load the truck. As he has on several occasions been very good about helping us, I donated the leather kit you sent me. I hated to part with it, but it has gone for good cause and I know it will be appreciated by the Jap but who will help us get food and tobacco for the men. I have stopped weighing myself. Why worry about weight when you can do nothing? I am sure I am quite thin. I started for the latrine today without my belt on and if I had not grabbed my shorts in time, I would've lost them. It is nice to be slender my age, but not that slender. News is good. Despite the starvation diet, morale is high.

July 11

Interesting figures show the attitude of the Filipinos. Our total purchases through Lt. Col. Johnson: February 1943 through June 1944; P902,685.23, our pay plus the Welfare Fund, same period; P586,556.00, showing a balance of P316,129.23 which has been sent into this camp. Of course, there's a lot yet unused in the hands of individuals, I believe at least 50,000.00. We were fortunate yesterday. We've received over 3500 kilos of panutsa so all will have something sweet for a while. The price; P13.80, is terrific, but as long as I can get money our little group or eat. We can settle afterwards. The new C.O. is really taking hold in a big way. Beginning last night everyone stands two roll call checks daily and the count is made by the Japanese C.O. Last night it was 9:45 PM before they completed the count. It is the first that the Japanese really knew, of their own knowledge, how many prisoners they had. The distribution of our mail has picked up. Nearly 400 yesterday. I will be lucky again soon with a letter from my love. I feel confident that there will be a lot of changes made here. I hope for the better.

July 13

Just as it looks that things are settling down with maybe a turn for the better, we're ordered to turn out a detail of 800 E.M., 16 officers, [1 F.O.], 6 Medical officers, 3 Chaplains, and 18 Med. E.M., to form five companies of 150 men and one of 89 with C.O. and Adjunct, leaving five officers available to command other companies raised elsewhere, probably Bilibid. They are to leave the 16th or shortly thereafter for Japan or Manchuria. Rains continue. The attached weight record is of interest. The officers listed are those who are, or were, on the staff. Today we receive a pair of socks, the first issued since about a year ago, February. One thing of interest is that as far as we can ascertain, no one from the Division #3, which is in the old hospital area [recently arrived from Davao] is to be on the detail.

The Colonel's Way

Names	Weight Jan 1-44	Present Weight	Loss
Lt. Col. Beecher	175	156	19
Lt. Col. Leinback	160	145	15
Lt. Col. Conaty	165	151	14
Lt. Col. Shreve	154	136	18
Lt. Col. Say	146	121	25
Lt. Col. Craig	175	150	25
Lt. Col. Brinkmeyer	181	170	11
Lt. Col. Brettel	165	143	22
Lt. Col. Cramer	154	136	18
Lt. Col. Drumond	165	146	19
Lt. Col. Johnson	165	145	22
Major Bradley	153	145	8
Major Houghton	178	150	28
Major Pysick	135	114	21
Major Reynolds	180	148	32
Major Maury	170	145	25

The Colonel's Way

DIARY THREE

{ July 15, 1944 – October 16, 1944 }

The Colonel's Way

The Colonel's Way

July 15, 1944

On the eve of my 47th birthday, I open a new book of entries of my life and work in the Philippines. This, the third, will be the last for it will take nearly a year to fill this, and it is my unfailing belief that the war will be over before that time elapses. Today, as I do many times, I reread your letters. Words fail me when I tried to describe the love an admiration I hold for you, my Judy mine. My only desire is to return to you, never to be separated again. I dream and pray every day that when this is all over I can return to you and retire from my service of my country to go to Our Decision, as we have so often planned, to live in happiness with our lads. The rain seems to be over. One third of the detail left at 5:00 AM today, being trucked to Manila. The second group [1/3] was due to leave by truck at noon. As we expected, they had set up a rather ambitious schedule for the trucks. It is now about 6:15 PM and the second group is just leaving. The third and last is now scheduled to go at 10:00 AM, the 16th, an all-night drive for our already over-tired drivers. It is amusing to see how the elaborate system of searching equipment and baggage has gone by the board when the pressure gets to the Japs. I am sorry to have to record the departure of Captain [Chap] Donald on this detail. He is a lot of fun and a fine morale builder – always cheerful.

July 16

Before I go to more serious things I will tell you of my birthday. I worked in my garden in the morning and after a shower, I wrote a card to you, my dearest. I hope it will reach you soon – when, I doubt. For dinner, to which Major Maury was invited, we have roast duck, the last I expect we will ever have here, delicious dressing and cucumbers from our garden. I was full for the first time in months. After a short nap, I went and played cribbage with Steve Sitter. Charlie Leinback and Maury both gave me an undershirt. All in all- a nice birthday in a prison camp. As to the camp, it is a madhouse. It was long after roll call [6:45 PM] before the detail was called to leave. When all the trucks were loaded there were 12 American POWs left over. The Adjunct [ours] was taking a bath so I answered the Japs call. I was told to feed and put them up for the night. When we thought things had quieted down some, one of the interpreters arrived with a request for a temporary detail of 180 men to leave a 10:00 AM today. We told him that was practically impossible and he left to report. Just after call to Quarters [9:00 PM] back comes a truck with 55 POWs. One truck had broken down so we had to get them taken care of. So things were when we went to bed. Early this AM we were told all leaving at noon. The truck for Manila will bring 80 POWs. When they arrived, there were 138 with 90 more to come when the truck returns tomorrow. What we will get, no one knows. From what we can get from the incoming men, the Japs are drawing from the detail working on the air fields on the island. The men were being sent to Bilibid and added to detail from there. Bilibid is full to overflowing. Our detail that left here late in June is still on a ship in the harbor with little or no water and two poor meals a day. Many sick are being disembarked and sent to the hospital at Bilibid. Manila is full of troops and the activity is feverish. The whole Jap garrison here seems very uneasy. It is a race against time. I hope they don't make it. Still no one being taken from Div. #3. Rumor has it that all over 40 are being rejected for Japan detail at Bilibid. The 180 will leave Tuesday.

July 19

Hard rains for the last two days. Our detail of 180 left yesterday at 2PM. Trucks to Cabanatuan, then train. All were soaking wet. 91 arrive from Bilibid the night of the 17th around 4:30 PM, 30 to our side and the remainder to Division #3, mostly officers. They had been in Bilibid Hospital. Since the trip up, all of the reports of the bad treatment on the trip are confirmed. Also, they were blindfolded and then tied in the trucks in rows parallel to the front of the body, ropes secured to the sides and kept that way during a 2 hour trip. Many fainted enroute. Our camp overhead has been cut, not out of proportion to our strength. However, no essential agencies deleted, but all cut. We have had no meat for a week. Today dried fish [local] have been supplied in limited quantities and, although hard to get by the nose, they are better than nothing. Our allowance is 15 g per man, per day –less than ½ ounce.

July 20

More rain but clear tonight. We were inspected today by two General officers. They were the Chief of the Supply Section [G-2] of the southern regions; the other, the General in charge of POW camps – Philippines. Their inspection was very cursory. They looked in two kitchens and passed through Division #1 and #2 on the way to the farm. No mail today. Our total so far is 18,385 in six months, less nine days.

July 21

Our fellow POWs now in the hospital area are to be transferred to our side. They are to go to Division#2, 736 in all, as follows: 43 Lt. Cols., 100 Majors, 157 Captains, 91 1st Lts., 99 2nd Lts., 7 Chief

The Colonel's Way

W.O. , 4 W.O., 102 NCOs, 127 Pvts., and one civilian. Lt. Col. Jonnie Woodbridge is among those listed. Joe Ganahl is quite sick with Bacillary dysentery and was taken to the hospital this PM. I went to see him and took him two eggs [duck at 1.90 ea.] I happen to have.

July 23

Today was just like Old Home week. So many officers we all knew who have been in Davao for nearly two years were in the group they came in today. They showed the effects of the trip as it was described earlier in these notes. 16 went directly to the hospital. Joe Ganahl is better. Friday night a company of Japs arrived in heavy marching order, about 200, not all equipped with rifles which leads us to believe they were Pioneer infantry or Engineers. They left by marching Saturday morning going east. News is good. Hitler is having internal troubles, the Russians are driving hard, and we are on Guam. I saw Jonnie Woobridge. Thin but okay.

July 25

The Japanese yesterday authorized us to increase our donation to Welfare Postal Savings, heretofore P50.00 from 100 field officers per month, to twice that sum. I assembled the newly arrived F.O. from Davao and explained the set-up. I am sure there will be no objection. Nearly all signed before I left, and authorization to have it deducted when their turn came to contribute. The Japs are preparing regulations to govern the camp. Johnson and I have prepared those governing the Commissary even down to the distribution of men in barracks. We, with Beecher's approval, are going to see that everyone, no matter what rank, gets his fair share of the essentials that we can get in, which, I am sorry to say, has not been so in many instances. Colonel Johnson [Comm.] was the one selected to send a radio home. They are broadcasting with a request that anyone picking up the message to relay it to the given address. He kindly mentions my name. I hope you receive word, my dearest, promptly. It is at least a hope that you will know I am okay in July 1944.

July 27

Still rain. We have hardly seen this on for two weeks. Quotations on beans [sack] reflects the decreasing value of the peso. Saturday last, P800; Monday, P850; Wednesday, P1000. All of the recently arrived Field Officers agreed to contribute to Welfare except three majors, Jackson [MC] Babcock and Webb. I made a trip to give them a second chance and to see if I could explain it further to them. They were extremely hostile, hardly condescending to listen to what I had to say. Your gifts to me [overnight kit] was graciously received by in my interpreter. I hate to part with it but it will do a no end of good where it is, and I can get along. Food is still the burning question. Everyone continues to go down in weight and resistance. Our hospital is filling up.

July 28

Not much change. Details are heavy, with lieutenant colonels required to work as laborers. Nice show with the Glee Club. Among others rendered was, "Among my Souvenirs", shades of the Columbia Club and lobster dinner with you. Fond memories. I slept badly. While I worked the garden today, I saw many of our men picking over the trash and garbage piles in hopes of finding something to eat. We live on hope.

The Colonel's Way

July 29

Your letter #18 arrived, the latest I have received. We will be in Ocean City together again someday, I know we will, my dearest. I learn was regret of the death of Lt. Gen. L. J. McNair today. He was killed in France. A great loss to the Nation and to us.

August 1

I was too excited to write in my book last night. The occasion: two wonderful letters from you, my Judy mine. # 19 and # 20. In the former, you spoke of your first word from me; in the latter, of your sending me a package. Something was censored out, followed by the words;" Taken April 4, 1942." I fear it refer to pictures which were not there. A letter from mother, September 8, gave news of the entire family, also spoke of someone's staying at the Plimhimmon, so I gather it was operating. I hope we are being paid. You are so smart to raise so much. I always fear that you work too hard. Rains continue and our little garden, on which we depend so much, does badly. We are to receive a draft from Bilibid, approximately 300, as follows; due in tomorrow at 4:00 PM; 100 hospital cases, 70 Quarters and 130 Duty. The Japanese have cut our camp overhead again. Their call for work detail was so great that we have had to turn out sick men lately. As this looks bad on the record, they are trying to cut our overhead. We may have to cut some of our entertainment programs. Needless to say, I did not sleep well last night. Too much lying awake dreaming of the days when we will be happy again.

The Colonel's Way

August 3

I have taken over the Camp Welfare, a fund of P10,000 subscribed by 200 Field Officers each month to purchase extra food for the sick, both in the hospital and in the Divisions. The actual cash is held by the Japanese Supply officer. I simply administer the fund. On the first, we had a flare-up of beatings on the farm. Personal investigation shows that a detail of mostly officers from Davao was assigned to carry litters of vegetables in from the farm, also leading them. Two of our supervisors warned them that they must load them well or there would be trouble. They failed to heed the warning and the Japs noticed it. This was in the morning. Immediately after lunch, the Jap farm officer, 2nd Lt. Kaseino, held a conference of his men, immediately followed by their going to where the same detail was working on the same work as the morning. They made the men load the litters to where they could hardly lift them and when, on the way in, the men began to play out, out came the clubs. We have protested. Food is terribly scarce. Our supper consisted of seven table spoonfuls of a mixture of rice, greens and fried fish and a small cookie.

August 4

In effect, we have had all rations cut again. Our standard ration has been 350 g rice, 150 g rice substitute [camotes at one time, shelled corn at another and recently rice as there were no rice substitutes available]. Today we had issued corn on the cob, in a proportion of 3 to 1 for 150 g of rice. We lost by test about 33 1/3%. Vegetables and fish remain the same. Weather is much better. Clear today except for the usual afternoon shower. Our mail deliveries are better, averaging over 350 per day this week. Beans are P1050 per sack.

August 7

As I stepped from our barracks in the pale morning moonlight, I was greeted with one of the most beautiful star displays I have ever witnessed. The eastern heavens just before dawn at this time of year contain our loveliest of constellations, in my opinion. We will look at them together, my dearest, some August morning as we leave our house and walk hand in hand eastward across our lawn. God willing, it may not be long. The Japs apologized for the beatings and promised that the litters would not be loaded in excess of 15 kilos per man. Bad news today. The men were discovered outside the sentry line on the airport. I doubt if they were trying to escape – simply trying to get out of work. Nice day with very little rain. I planted about 450 to 500 radish seeds that the Japs gave us. We also got onion, cabbage, tomato, mustard greens and some others. Onion and radish are all that we will grow during the rains. The European situation seems to be clearing fast. It is sure to have great repercussions in this theater.

August 8

Our troubles are mostly gastronomical. Survey made on the sixth shows 1099 cases of nutritional edema out of a strength of 2860 in Division's # 1 and #2. While in the hospital area this morning, I was told by the surgeon that they had six cases of impacted bowels, all due to many eating corn cobs. All had to be operated on. Our noon meal due to shortage of rice is now what is called lugao [soft rice gruel] with greens, corn, okra, or what other filling is available. Very unappetizing, as the iron pot and the vegetables give it a deep gray color. It is all we have so we eat it. The men who were discovered outside the sentry line at the airport got 10 days in the Jap guardhouse. They were not abused.

The Colonel's Way

August 10

Last night, another wonderful letter, your#7, Feb. 28, 1943. I get a little more homesick, if possible, and lie awake daydreaming each time one arrives. They are so welcome and, my dearest, you are so brave and fine. You speak so of our boy's father. Don't forget their mother while you are putting out bouquets. The place must be lovely. You have done so much. From your remark about the well, our supply must be problematical. We may have to drill. Rain, the order of the day, however, I fixed a bed and planted some Japanese radishes. Today they are up. More dried fish have come in. Although we are always hungry and terribly thin we are in no danger of starvation. The fish, about 3 inches to 4 inches long, sun dried, are first fried then ground and added to our rice; heads, scales, bones and all, 15 g per man per day.

August 11

Tragedy stalked through camp, for today around 2:00 PM, I was awakened by Major Reynolds [Adjunct] to be told that a man had been shot by the Japanese sentry in Div. #2. Lt. Robert Huffcut, Signal Corp, AUS., was the victim. [Huffcut was an ex-member of the Philippine High Commissioners staff, expert on economics and considered one of the ablest young men in the State Department. He was in his late twenties; a Ph.D. Columbia University. He had refused to leave with Sayer[?], his duty being here]. I have yet to make a full investigation but all indications are that he was shot while picking okra in his garden inside the inner fence. This, the Japanese deny, claiming that he was on the guard path, which is off limits. I believe that testimony will refute that claim. Some sun today, but rain now. My supper, seven spoons of rice with fish and a rice cookie.

August 13

Sunday, I did not go to church. Our Communion service has been discontinued and I cannot go to long sermons with which the non-sectarian services are blessed. Investigation of shooting is not yet complete. I had a nice talk with Captain George Kaufman [Cav. Res.] who lives in Jersey. He has had experience in remodeling old houses, having done the last of which he was occupying when called to the colors. He gave me some very good advice especially as to the materials, their purchase, etc, and also what agreements it is best to make with carpenters, plumbers, etc. He advised to buy all plumbing from Sears, also stoves, set for kitchen, lumber. He believed little could be saved and the same with electrical fixtures, cable or conduit, yes. He advised allowing each carpenter, plumber, electrician to purchase some of the materials so he can realize some profit. The chances are he will do little nicer job. Time and materials to be a basis of all work. Contracts are bad as you always want to make some slight changes and then you pay dearly.

August 14

Detail call to leave the 17th, 500 EM, 5 Officers, 2 Medical Officers and 10 Medical Corps, EM. I had expected it despite details of the difficulty of Japanese shipping to leave Manila. Our returns show about 560- odd well men for duty. We will have to dig deep. Still no indication of Officer details, labor is what they seem to want. Nice letter from Bill Shreve, March of 1943. The Japs are determined that there will be no escape. Today orders were issued that details, except truck drivers and wood detail, would go without shoes. Brutal on our people who are not accustomed to it.

The Colonel's Way

Rains continue and my garden, on which we depend so much, does poorly.

August 15

By a great good fortune we received some meat and bones today, a present from Mr. Ted Lewen who works on the Jap side. It is wonderful to feel satisfied after a meal. Last evening Lt. Yamji and Maceda [interpreter] came with instructions from the Major that not enough men were turned out for details and then in the future everyone, regardless of position, would have to do some work, i.e., on the farm. All of these orders are, of course, met with arguments by Major Reynolds.[The following pages are torn].

```
Conference; Major Takasaki
August 16, 1944
```

```
Major Takasaki: The kitchen crew - the number of
people now being used in the place seems to me
too many and I will study it again and tell you
the exact number of people you can use in the
kitchen. If anybody is found in the barracks who
was not authorized to any duty approved by us,
such a man will be punished and also the barracks
leader or responsible people for that man, will
also be punished.
     The reason why I want to strictly carry
out my intentions under the present circumstances
is that every country in the world is now in the
war and everybody must work to live and everybody
is actually working in those countries.  As you
don't read a newspaper, you have no knowledge,
but we have knowledge that in the States all
people are under the same situation.  We have
classifications of the ration for those who work
and for those who don't work and I strictly
adhere to the regulations. I will give them a
share of food according to the rules.
```

The Colonel's Way

We reduce the amount of fuel in the kitchens and I notice that the kitchens here are burning too much wood and you people must notify the kitchen crew to economize the use of wood as much as possible. The boundary line on the east side of this camp will be fixed and the order will be established from today and we will provide some sticks and wire to show clearly the boundary. Unfortunately, an officer was shot to death the other day, but we will try to fix the line clearly. All people must be aware of the boundary line.

You have eight latrines which are outside of the new boundary line and these will be moved and the work is to be done by the men who are using that particular latrine. There is a small drain ditch between the latrine in the barracks and the new plan of the boundary will be along the drain ditch to their. Although you will utilize the materials that are put now on the latrines, like boxes, we know the material will be insufficient to make new latrines and we will issue material needed for the new ones.

I have some definite news from my people that there are some Americans made prisoner that have such an opinion that the more they work, the more they will benefit the Japanese army, so they want to be idle, but this is strictly prohibited by me and from now on, if anybody is found to have such an opinion and do in such a way, I will punish him very seriously, very severe. I hope that such news is a groundless rumor in this camp and all people have no such opinion in this camp and all things will be carried out smoothly.

This is all am going to talk to you today and all my men must be notified - everybody in the camp must know the things that I told you and there will be nobody who was not notified about these matters which I told you now; without exception each individual must be notified about these matters. If there are any questions among you, I will give you time.

Q. By Lt. Beecher: Now, in regard to the latrines - may we use the present latrine -at

The Colonel's Way

least some of them until we get others build and shift them over? As I say, the work is started and we will get it done just as soon as we possibly can and until we get that done, there is no place for them to go.

A. As the boundary line work will be started from today, when the new latrines are ready for use, we will issue orders and you may use the old ones until then.

Q. by Major Reynolds: The Majors orders will be published at and evening roll call tonight which is the first assembly.

A. by Mr. Maceda: You must be very careful to notify everybody and not only one time and you must repeat it. Some may be on duty and you must find that everyone is notified about it. Any other questions?

Major Takasaki: I am open to receive any suggestions or anything which you want to request of the Japanese authorities and you can suggest or bring any matters which can be done to improve the present condition of the camp. I will thoroughly go through the whole matter brought by you. While I was in the office in Davao, I appointed one or two days a week for all men for work, both Japanese and American side, irrespective of their work, busy or not. One doctor told the Japanese Authority; 'I am on Medical duty and I'm doing enough for one man and if I go out on the farm, my duty is doubled and with this I do not agree.' To carry out our plan on the Japanese side will be order of the day and every Japanese soldier an officer has his own duty, even the Major has an assigned duty, but will be on a farm for duty; the same thing as all the rest of men do. It is my opinion that one man who all the time sits in the office may spoil this health and one day on the farm or field will be very good and also is a matter of principle – if one doesn't work, he cannot get any food. The regular details on the farm whenever they see the

staff members on the same job, they are very
pleased and are naturally impressed that they are
cooperating with each other and the effect is
very good. This is also very beneficial that
staff members see sometimes on the field what
kind of labor and what kind of work they're doing
on the farm so that they can see personally and
check up on any kind of things outside.

[Major Takasaki's talk was interpreted by Mr.
Maceda]

August 17

Our detail left this AM at 9:00 marching. At the last minute the Japs C.O. ordered that the men would have to carry their baggage. He said, "I inspected the baggage yesterday and the men did not have too much, now they have padded it so I will not give them transportation." The truck with the American Officers baggage and the Japs soldiers, went out half empty. Planning on having their things sent by truck as heretofore, much was not packed to carry and there was no time to repack. Dozens of men lost all they had. No clothes, shoes, mess gear, blankets or canteens were issued. We were told to get blankets [shortage of 106] and shoes [shortage 73] from the men in camp. The Japanese are terribly short of everything. The supplies needed for the latrines are not forthcoming regardless of the fact that we were ordered today to have them for finished in four days. In view of the order that all details go barefoot and according to the threat in Major Takasaki's talk, I go without shoes each afternoon if I have to hit the farm. My feet will be used to it. To date we have received 25,396 letters, seven months average per month; 3628.

The Colonel's Way

<u>August 19, 1944</u>

I had my heart and blood pressure checked, all okay. I am very fortunate. Another detail of 4 Med. officers, 10 of Medical EM, one Chaplain and 65 W.O., or enlisted. We believe that it is a fill up for some outside detail on this island. Destination we believe- Japan.

```
Conference: Major Takasaki
Place: Division II Office

Attendance:
     Staff Members
     Division Commanders
     Hospital Commander
     Division Adjuncts
     Hospital Adjunct

Interpreter: Mr. Maceda
Speaker:[unless otherwise noted] Maj. Takasaki
```

The reason why I ordered you to assemble here today is that this is a plan for using many of the war prisoners which will be important to you. There will be very few people in this camp. There will be much reduction in the personnel of this camp. It will mean that prisoners of war will be self-supporting, to work themselves and to produce the food by themselves. The amount of produce here is not sufficient and up to now we have been buying from the market as much as possible, but recently there's very little that you can buy in the market and things are becoming short every day. From now on we all have to depend upon our own products which will be produced on our farm. I found that comparatively we have too many patients and too many weak men compared to the number of healthy men in this camp. So from now on, we must utilize all healthy men irrespective of age, office, or any kind. They must all go out and be engaged in the producing of our food. So we must now find out how to get the labor strength. Up to now, all of the permanent quarters have been permitted to stay in the camp, but from now on the event they we must you Allies. If one person has not perfect legs, he must use his hands; if he has not perfect hands, he must use is feet. Upon my arrival in this camp I first noticed that in this camp we have too many staff members and too many kitchen crews, so I have planned to reduce those personnel. Unless otherwise noted, we can take out as many as are necessary for the farming. I have this plan in mind ever since I arrived at this camp, but I could not spare any time to discuss this matter and now I have a chance I want to go into this matter with you. If you will talk with Colonel Olsen of Camp #2; you will find the details or an outline of my plans there. I have decided the number of staff members and will now tell you. All men take out paper and note down what I say.

The Staff members and Office clerks in groups, in POW Office, the total number of personnel has been 11, and this number will remain unchanged. In each division we will provide one group commander and two adjuncts and one assistant adjunct, a total of four in each division.

Typist —the total until now – two officers and 12 enlisted men – that means total 14, and this number will be reduced from now on to 7 men.

In Camp Commissary we had 4 officers and 1enlisted man – I mean the Camp and Division commissary -we have 4 officers and 1 enlisted man; in total we had 5, but this number will be reduced to 2 men, so 2 men means the regular commissary staff. But when we receive delivery and you need additional hands, we will permit some extra number of men.

Rational Staff— the Supply Department – we had 6 officers and 5 enlisted men, total 11 men; but this category will be entirely closed out and we can use nobody for that department.

The Colonel's Way

In the Details office we had 5 officers and 3 enlisted men; the total we have had: 8 men; but this department will be also closed; that means nobody will work. The work of Supply and Details office will be handled by those 11 in the POW Office.

Supply matters will be handled entirely in the POW Office and the figures will be transmitted to the Division Headquarters staff who will handle the work. In Camp II we had 2,800 men and all the work of this kind was handled by Colonel Olson and 3 more men; that is, they handled all the work for 2,800 men.

Utility Office-at present we have 12 officers and 11 enlisted men, a total we have of 23 men. We will carry on this number of men unchanged for the time being.

Shoe cobblers and tailors- at present we have 1 officer and 8 enlisted men- a total of 9. This number will be changed. For barbering purposes we have some number of men. In the working day, all people are supposed to be engaged in their own work and this item will be canceled and people will have their hair cut doing their rest time.

In the Wage Account Office-2 officers and 1 enlisted man and this number will remain unchanged.

The Chicken Coop - one man and this will remain.

The Library Department - we have 2 officers and 1 enlisted man, a total of 3. This will also remain unchanged.

Chaplains - 4, we have had 5 men, but we agree to 4 men from now on.

The Kitchen Crew - we have had 96 men in total, officers and enlisted men, but from now on there will be **6** officers and **80** enlisted men, a total of **86** men.

The Company Leaders - we have **16** men and Assistant Company Commanders; **17** men, and we will carry on these figures, but you must send out for work half of them each day - that means we must have about **16** or **17** more for the work and you can use the men by reliefs.

The Runners – we have had **4** runners up to now, but this will be revised to **2** and runners will belong to POWs.

We have had Unloaders or so called 'stand by' detail – **50** men but this item will be entirely cancelled and will be sent out for farm work. When necessary, we will direct you to take out the necessary number of men.

Now for the Hospital: the Medical Hdqtrs. in this group; we have at present **2** Medical officers and **4** Medical Corps men, a total of **6** and this number is unchanged. In the hospital there will be no changes in the fixed personnel and dispensaries in Div. I and Div. II; the number of personnel are unchanged at this time. The total number is unchanged in the Medical department, both in the Hospital and in the Group; but I will study the situation – that means **211** men – and I will still go into this matter further and when I form some idea to reduce the personnel, I will do that. Is that clear to you? You can figure out the revise number of personnel of over- head, can you? The assignment and selection of men we will do in the Japanese Hdqtrs. In the future, there will be new joinings from the outside – that means from Camp II and other detail places and whenever we can find some capable officer for the work of any kind on this side, I will assign them to the job.

All of the American prisoners in Camp **#1** and Camp **#2** are under my jurisdiction and if you face some trouble in the assignment of men, I can do it myself. Seeing this camp, some things are very good and some are not very good in comparison with Camp II, so any matters that require improvement, I will carry on the improvement gradually.

Generally speaking, the setup and Camp II has been better than this camp; that is my impression. In the Work Office System and also the system of distribution of food, it is my definite opinion that Camp II was better than here and you have to study still more to find out ways to accurately and quickly do the work. Colonel Beecher, you can express your opinion whether it is possible to operate with a number of personnel I have given you.

Answer by Colonel Beecher:

Under the circumstances I can express no opinion at present because I haven't had an opportunity to try what has been ordered. However, we will do our best. It will require a re- organization and before expressing any opinion, I would have to make the re-organization in accordance with the order and express an opinion it if it can be done.

Statement by a Major Takasaki:

Since the Fall of Bataan I have been engaged in the matter of war prisoners and the figures I now give to you have some basic foundation according to my experience, and I think it possible to operate by that number of people, so I order you to revise the number of men. Naturally, I realize that the amount of work assigned one person will be increased, but I feel confident that people can do the work satisfactorily. However, as Colonel Beecher told me now, after you try to operate this camp by that number of people, if you feel some inconvenience and in some cases you find it impossible, I will be glad to consider your opinion, but have to try it a couple of weeks and you will complete the reorganization during today, and tomorrow you submit us a list of members. On the list we need the names of the officers, wherever officers are assigned, and enlisted men we do not need any names. To the staff members and also the kitchen crew, considering the amount of work they do, I realize that they work the same labor as on the farm, so from this evening I will agree to issue a cow. When the assignment is completed, we will provide an armband on each staff member showing the assigned duty. Also the kitchen crew will have an armband. The reason why we provide armbands is to segregate the duty men from the general men. Approximately two days in the week we have agreed to do the distribution of commissary articles. I will make more definite about a cow - all overhead men will receive A cow. Naturally those patients or quartered cases, if they don't work, they will depend upon all only the regular cow - that is the B cow. Tomorrow the Japanese side is going to celebrate the opening of the second year of this camp and in memory of that, for your side, we will issue a cow and tobacco to you. Tomorrow we will be holding the celebration outside the fence and if you would like to do something in memory of those people who died in this camp, you can conduct some assembly at the same time, but the time must be reported to Japanese headquarters. In the graveyard in this camp, I find that there are many grasses, very tall, not so neat, so I issued orders to the Japanese officer to make the place more clean and on the appointed day of cleaning some of the officers, if they care to go, can go out together with a grass cutters detail and can do something there. Not so big number, only limited number of men can go there. It is my idea, four or five men may be all right. That is all.

August 20

Sunday. Yesterday we [staff group C.O. and Adjuncts] were called to another conference with the Jap commander. His remarks ably taken down by my part time clerk, M/ Sgt. Harrison of the 200 CAG [AA] is attached. Today, as promised, we receive the Cow [1] or about 1 pound of meat and bone for 10 men, also the tobacco, four small leaves per man. Our usual issue of cigarettes, 10 per week, was cut to four. I believe this was a coincidence and not premeditated. We held a brief memorial service at 9:00 AM fairly well attended. I presided. This will not be complete without some record of the condition of the men and officers of the camp. I believe a very critical stage, for from the air the Philippines have been attacked. We will, I believe, either go to Japan or be in a fair way to being delivered in from to 60 to 90 days. Everyone is terribly thin. On the 13th of August there were 514 permanent disabilities in Division #1 and #2; 597 a marked 'Quarters' for minor in ailments up to and including pneumonia, and 587 patients in the hospital. Our total strength that day: 3543. Men are continually being beaten for stealing and eating vegetables on the farm, but continue to take the chance. I saw three men today sitting in the mud and rain, waiting for the Jap guardhouse in hope of getting the leftovers. One captain from the 86th F.A. [PS] told me that while on detail caring for the Japanese ducks, he was able to steal three mess kits of the cooked duck food and eat it. Tempers are short and nerves on edge. Not a day passes that we do not have fights, mostly over trifles. Hopes are still high and no one wants to go to Japan.

August 22

Another wonderful letter from you, # 12, written on Mother's day, May 9, 1943. I did get a laugh about our Sandy boy and his spelling. I have never learned, as these notes will bear witness. But it has not been a handicap. I am sure it will not be for him. A letter from mother, December, 1942, telling of Bill Shreve. Good for him. I hope he is a lieutenant colonel by now. We were each issued a coconut on Sunday last, and another today and there are a good quantity still to go to the messes. Colonel Johnson was told by the Japs Supply officer that these and the tobacco issued Sunday were bought with the 3% which we pay on commissaries. The camp now falls in front of the POW headquarters in mass twice a day, rain or shine, to be checked by the Jap O.D. It takes about 55 minutes and only the sick, too ill to move, and the hospital are excused. Our poor, under- fed, almost naked men take a bad beating in the cold rain and the chill before dawn. Faintings are regular.

August 25

Time marches on and every day I am closer you, my dearest Judy. Yours of September 6, #21, the latest I have received. Also, one from mother, Aug. 17th. Darling, you speak of being the wife that I put my trust in. My Judy, if I thought I had been able to do my job here as well as I know you have done yours, I would be very happy. Not much change. We are to be inspected tomorrow by Jap C.O. Only people with armbands [authorized overhead] and the sick are supposed to be in camp. If any others are found, Division C.O. and all concerned are to be punished. Our Red Cross medicines for August and September arrived the 23rd. They are held in Manila and given to us every month. We are back on Vita-caps until October 1.

```
Prisoner of War Office
Military Prison Camp No. 1 of the Philippine
Islands, Cabanatuan, P.I.

COPY:  Aug. 26, 1944

SUBJECT: Increase in Welfare contribution
```

The Colonel's Way

TO: Commanding Officer, Military Prison Camp No. 1 of the Philippine islands, Cabanatuan, P.I.

1. It is respectfully requested that the amount of money authorized for expenditure for the welfare of sick prisoners of war be increased to P22,500 per month, this amount to be collected by contribution of P75.00 each month from 300 Field officers who have signified their willingness to such contributions.

2. At present there are in this camp many prisoners of war who have been returned to this camp either through the Military hospital at Bilibid, Manila, or directly from outside work details, due to the failing condition of their health. As the health of the men in this category has improved, they have subsequently been sent on other details, leaving in this camp the more serious cases.

3. At present time of 458 sick prisoners of war are being given additional food, consisting of 50 g of beans each day. The cost of beans for one month at existing prices is approximately P12,540. This leaves no funds available for the purchase of fresh fruit and eggs which are sorely needed in the hospital for patients recovering for operations and those in the tuberculosis ward.

4. During the month of December 1942, when the sick fund was authorized beans cost P36.25 per sack[25 gantas] duck eggs, 9 ½ centavos each and bananas 85 centavos per 100. At the present time beans cost P$1100.00 per sack, or 30 times as much; duck eggs, P$2.35 each, or about 25 times greater; bananas, P28.66 per 100, more than 33 times as much.

> 5. There are almost 1200 prisoners of war who are either patients in the hospital or temporarily sick marked 'quarters' in Division I. and II. at the present time. This figure does not include many permanent disability cases who would be benefited by extra food were unavailable.
> 6. If this increase is authorized, it will only be expended only for the welfare of the sick as shown above.

> Arthur L. Shreve
> Lieutenant-Colonel, GSC
> Morale and Welfare Officer

August 26

As you see by the enclosed above we are trying to get the Welfare fund increased. Our verbal request was turned down. Pay is to be increased for workers from August 10 - 20¢ for Pvts., 25¢ for NCOs, 35¢ for Warrants – per 6 hour day and increase of 10¢. For salaried personnel P500 increase per month.[Note paragraph four] I am a little downcast tonight. It is the treatment, according to my fellow officers and men. <u>No shoes</u>. All ranks, including lieutenant colonels, are doing all sorts of menial work for the Japs, officers cleaning around the Guard Co., kitchen and quarters, carrying slops and cleaning around latrines. I am fortunate to be on staff. I take no chances; I go without shoes all afternoon each day just in case.

August 27

Sunday. The camp is rife with rumors today. The Japs asked for list by numbers of well officers, enlisted men and Medical E.M.

The talk is, of course, of a large detail to Japan. Who knows? A lovely day spent just doing nothing and visiting. Joe Ganahl came down with some letters from this family. He is a fine man, cheerful and optimistic, though troubled with a skin infection that has been chronic since he has been a prisoner. News is good. Germany, I hope, will not last out September.

August 29

Things about the same, except the food. I feel that I should be braying like a mule for I have had practically nothing but corn for, it seems, days. We are receiving a scant 350 g of rice, the rice substitute is corn, the vegetable issue is corn, and the extra work ration is corn. We have had boiled ground corn for breakfast and lunch for two days and hominy. For work ration, a little rice with fish gravy and more hominy for supper. Taste no longer matters – only food.

August 30

Conference with Camp C.O., Beecher, myself, Johnson, North [Hospital C.O.], Craig [Medical chief]. Much to our surprise and in reply to our request, he upped the Welfare to P18,000 and said that there would soon be more officers joining the camp. When they arrived he would authorize an additional P2000. Lucky me- four letters, two from you and two from Bill. All 25 words, not so nice, but welcome.

September 2

No entry for three days partially due to stomach attack and partially due to my being very busy. My attack was due, I think, to

The Colonel's Way

too much corn. I am well over it now. On the morning of the 31st after being up sick nearly all night, I was called to Jap headquarters for a conference with the C.O., reference: welfare. He discussed with me the amounts and the number of officers in each grade to contribute. Result: Colonels and Lt. Cols.- P50.00; Majors- P40.00; Captains- P15.00. We collected our P18,000, though it was hard work getting all the captains to sign the authority for deduction by 7:00 PM September 1, when they were paid, 408 in all. On September 1 we were called to furnish a detail of six Line officers, 20 Medical officers, two Chaplains, 48 Medical E.M.s, 336 E.M.s or civilians. 200 of them left today at 11:00 AM, including one special Medical officer not included in the original draft. The remainder will leave at 7:00 AM, September 3 - all classed as Disability. We are very low in enlisted, now only in key positions in messes, and clerks. Officers perform all other duties: runners, cut wood, carry rations, police and sanitary details. Although our patient strength has increased, our hospital has been out 8 officers and 12 E.M. Medical Corps. Chap. Taylor from Special Prisoner to Hospital; four remaining; Lt. Col. Mack, Capt. Aton, Civ. Threatt and Rogers. We are no longer allowed to furnish them with tobacco or books. I have read the report of investigation by our J. A.G., Major P. Koster. It is too voluminous to make a part of this record. Lt. Huffcut was certainly inside of the limits set by the Japs. Lt. Tasuino; Imperial Japanese Army, was in temporary command of the camp. Witnesses: Lt. Col. W.R. Craig, CAC, USA; Corp. Rufus H. Turnbow; [1-8018186], 60 C.A.C Bn., S.C.; Raymond F. Hoffman, U.S. Navy; 1st Sgt. Louis M. Hix, Btry. 'H', 50th CAC, USA; M/Sgt. Joe G. Collier, 48 Mat. Sq., Air Corps; Maj. William A. Gay, C.E., USA.

September 6

On September 3 we received from Bilibid 98 officers and men, a large percentage of which were sent to the hospital. There were eight British soldiers among them, captured in the Singapore campaign. They are in pretty bad shape, 44 days on shipboard, poor food and little water. Rations increased, fish for all, from 20 to 30 g. Workers, 20 g extra. It will be a wonderful help if we can get it. We are out of sugar and sugar substitute. It is hard without something sweet no matter how little. I was fortunate to get some extra money enabling me to get a few duck eggs. I had two for supper. They were P4.00 each. For what I had to pay for the money, they cost me $4.00 for the two. What is money when your life depends on a little extra food? Good news. France and Belgium are free. Holland invaded. We hope each day for action here.

September 7

God in his mercy has allowed the Special Prisoners to be released. There were only four left: Col. Mack, Captain Aton, Civ. Threatt and Rogers. They were all admitted to the hospital. Threatt was the sickest with diarrhea. I believe that the Japs were anxious for their health. Six grand letters, one from you my love, three from Bill, one Rosalie, and one from Uncle Henry, so nice of him. I see Warren is a member of the firm. Hot dry days. Our extra fish can be noticed, although only a spoonful.

September 11

Dividends were collected this morning on my going without shoes, for this was the day selected by the Jap C.O. for the staff in the

The Colonel's Way

camp overhead to go to the farm. We lined up, were counted out, and waited for about 45 minutes until they Major arrived. He gave us a speech about everyone in the world today had to work or starve, and that we must work hard. Beecher and Division C.O. and Adjunct were withdrawn and we marched to an old cornfield where some of us cut stalks while the remainder pulled the stubble in the weeds. I did well – no fatigue, no blisters, only minor cuts from cogon grass. After we got in we found that Beecher, etc., all were taken on a grand tour, their bare feet nearly killing them. Officers placed on Welfare, as they are all paid, are required to pay for what they receive up to half the pay of the company grade pay [P35.00]. All we really give them is a priority on food at a reduced price. So little comes in, especially beans, that they all go to Welfare. I collected P433.00 and tried to deposit this with the Japs to the credit of the fund but it was too much for them to understand. So we gave up trying and will collect and use the money and not put it through the books.

September 13

Another death. One of the patients in the dysentery area died. He developed and pneumonia yesterday and although he had plenty of sulfur, he did not react. The Japs are digging in. Last night until after dark and today, the office force has been working on fox holes. At each corner of the compound and at each guardhouse they have, or are building, huge redouts, I believe for no good purpose, as their will in my opinion be but little fighting here ever if we, the POWs, are here during the campaign. Of course, we are getting in close. I believe the Japs have a right to feel nervous. A nice letter [25 words] from Bill. I feel fine, sleeping better, believe I am gaining a little. Our fish ration for workers is back.

The Colonel's Way

September 16

Our wedding anniversary – 18 years. All too short, except the last three, which without you, my dearest have seemed without end. But there is always that hope that soon it will be all over and we can be united again. You are always in my thoughts, day again and again, as I once said to my mother; the best and the most wonderful thing that ever happen to me was Judy McCoy. My hopes are high, dears, Providence provided me with a letter from my love, your # 31, November 18, and the news is good. We have occupied the last two Jap bases, moving the forces to within less than 500 miles. Next year, for sure. I love you.

September 20

Another detail called late the night of the 16th, 2 Chap., 10 doctors, 30 Medical Corps enlisted. They left by truck early Monday the 18th. Little has transpired. Days followed days with little change. I had two wonderful letters from you today. A long one, #11, April 21, 1943. Dearest mine, how proud I am of you. Your cheerful letters, so interesting about our place which we love, never a word of complaint. It is terribly hard not knowing if I am alive or dead. It is different here. We have a constant fight against disease, lack of food and the all present menace of the Japs. Yours is harder to endure than mine, my darling, and you are doing it splendidly.

September 21

My darling, long remembered will be today, for this morning from the east over the mountains came our Navy planes. The first flight, of about 35 single engine bombers escorted by fighters flying high, came into view about 9 to 9:30 AM. The bombers in beautiful formation, the fighters covered them on all sides from a greater altitude. Of course, there was much speculation, but as they passed over just south of us and we could distinctly hear the fighters clear their guns, I was sure they were ours. Flight followed flight, mostly south of us. Still many were not convinced until one flight returned eastward dropping four fighters to strafe the airfield near camp. There was one unfortunate Jap in the air near the field or over camp, crashed and burned on the edge of the farm. This afternoon they came again. I believe in the five flights I saw there were over 300. As one flight returned, two fighters dropped out, swung over us and fired their guns in salute. Our men behaved beautifully! No cheers, just big grins. The Japs were a bit stumped, doubled the guard and called in all work details except woodcutters. What a day!

September 22

Our Navy aviators came again this morning at 7:30 AM, flying high over the mountains in formation. They strafed and bombed [small bombs] the field near here. Sometimes I have felt a little ashamed of the way we took cover in the early days of the war, but my heart glows with pride at our conduct as compared with these Japs. When the field was hit we were all watching and continued to do so. Jap headquarters, 100 yards away, was cleared in 10 seconds. The guards in the guardhouse all went to ground. One chap tried to get his tin hat on with pour success. He finally threw it away in disgust and jumped in a fox hole which was full of water. They successfully lured one of our hosts' chickens through the fence. In 4 seconds he was in a bag- in 4 hours in us. Chicken soup, boiled chicken, corn bread and the regular fish and rice. I am really full. We await impatiently news of the raid we have been witnessing.

The Colonel's Way

September 23

The score for the first day was received late last night. The Japs took a bad beating – 110 planes shot down, 95 on the ground, 11 ships sunk, 26 probables. We lost only 15 planes the first day. Ration cut, 100 g rice, 50% of cooking fat. 50 extra grams of corn in lieu thereof.

September 26

The total for the raid have been made public. Second day, better than the first. High hopes of delivery here as the Japs have lost so much shipping. The wood detail has been discontinued. The Japs will, according to them, will supply the fire wood for the camp. Good indication?

September 27

Two letters from you, my love,# an 33 #and #39. Len is in Europe, I gather. Long conference with Beecher as to the Jap capabilities and plans to meet them. I believe we have left no stone unturned. Ito and Hitage [interpreters] left today to go near Manila, our G-2, Los Banos, where our late C.O. and Adjunct are. We expect that all but seriously ill will be sent there from Bilibid.

October 3

I dreamed of letters from my love last night and awakened to find three from her beside my plate. Wonderful messages of love and cheer. Your courage and devotion, darling, know no end. Our commissary expenditures are limited this month to P80,000 – not to include Welfare. The Jap wood detail that came in at 5:00 PM today as I was awaiting supper had 26 men with rifles, 16 men with axes, and the Philippines are their Allies in a war against us? Last Sunday [October 1] two trucks arrived just prior to supper. From them where unloaded 64 white men, no shoes, practically no clothes, unshaven, dirty, and unmistakably many sick. They were accompanied by an officer and a detail of Japs who had left here two or three days ago. They were checked and counted and turned to us for shelter and food. 18 Dutch and 46 British POWs. They were, as far as the Japs knew, the survivors of 1200 who left for Singapore about three months ago. We got blankets, mess gear, blue denims and shoes for them from Lt. Yamaji. I passed the hat for them and got cigarettes and soap for them that night. In the morning, in response to the call, I was swamped with soap, razors, toothbrushes, combs, towels, handkerchiefs, etc. The response was terrific and our new comrades were overcome with gratitude. Briefly, their story as told by Lt. Zonneveld, Dutch East Indian Army, is as follows: After the fall of the Indies he and other Dutch and British POWs were sent by boat and marching to Thailand [Siam] to build a railroad connecting Burma with French Indo-China. Of 45,000, about 25,000 died of cholera. After the completion of the road they were returned via Singapore where they were put on a boat [1200 to 1000 British, 200 Dutch] and started north. They were eight weeks on route to Manila. They lay in the harbor there for about a month during which time about 90 British and 4 Dutch died. Fresh water was scarce, two meals a day [rice] with about 20 to 40 g of dried fish once a week. During this period the ship moved many times to small base and other places in Manila Bay. As part of a large convoy they left on September 20. On the morning of the 21st, off the Zambales coast, somewhere between Subic Bay and Ibe, the Lieutenant was on the after well deck. He heard and saw planes, but believing them Jap, paid no attention and did not realize that they were Allied until M.C.

bullets began to hit the ship. Two bombs hit, near misses near the stern, one starboard, one port. The next one hit the engine room and the next one, one of the forward hatches where the British were. He went below, got his life belt and started his men topside. When he arrived on deck the boat was only a foot out of water and had been hit by a third bomb. He stepped into the water and the ship went down before he had swum 10 yards. He was in the water 4 ½ hours and estimates that they were 4 kilometers from shore. He saw 3 cargo and one destroyer go down. Others he believed sunk, but did not see them. He saw a Jap destroyer pick-up Jap survivors and leave POWs in the water. On one life raft there were two POWs, two Japs and a pig. The destroyer picked up the Japs and the pig. When they got to shore that Jap beach defense made no effort to help them through the surf. They were put in a house, told that all the American planes had been shot down and no one was allowed outside. He heard planes all the next day. They were fed by Filipinos two meals a day –stew with meat and rice and later, at his request, vegetables were added. They were there 10 days. Cigarettes, clothes and food were supplied by natives only. They told him if he had come at night, they would've hidden them all. Lt. Zonneveld estimates that from 300 to 325 got to shore.

October 5

I awakened this morning to find your #40, March, and enclosed was my Judy. Oh darling, you cannot know the joy your picture brought and so like my fondest memories. Socks, saddle shoes, skirt and sweater, even the cigarette and the way you hold it. You look so well my love, no change <u>my Judy</u>. Two weeks ago today and our aviators have not returned and with each passing day the question – if they do not come again soon, will the Japs send this to Japan? I'm going to try and duplicate all of my important papers so if we do go, I can put them with these notes which will be buried, assuring your getting them if I should not return.

October 6

Caloric value of the ration as figured by our Medical headquarters: Reg. ration, 1760 – workers, 892 additional- 4 sick in the hospital, 46 additional - seriously ill in the hospital, 140*[*canned milk].

October 8

Many happy returns of the day, my darling Judy. God bless and keep you. You've brought to me only happiness and I love you with all my heart. To say that I am proud of you it's just a limitation placed on our language. In you there is that rare combination of being always my sweetheart and a fine and a devoted mother to our boys. If by some un-luck chance I fail to return from this adventure I hope you will keep our place in Howard. Our boys, I know will, under your loving care, grow into fine honorable gentleman, God- fearing, and with a love and devotion to their country. I confidently expect to tell you all this and lots more in not too long a time, but I'm writing this just in case. You are in my thoughts all day and I dream of you after lunch. Your picture is a great joy.

October 9

At 8:00 PM last night a detail was called – 250 EM, 150 Line officers and two Chaplains. Half of it left at 9:00 today, the remainder to leave on the 10th, same time. Many are downcast. Believe we will all be shipped to Japan at once. I do not believe so. I still have hope of being here "Come the Yanks".

The Colonel's Way

October 13

My darling, today and may well be the day that marks the turning point in this war for us. Could well be that it may send me into your arms fully a year sooner for the Yanks were here again. We did not see so many. Clouds were low, but since early this morning when we saw all our planes, we have heard from time to time the deep throated of roar of many American planes. Yesterday the Japs gave out the figure of those to stay: 17 officers and men to work for the Japs, 400 patients in the hospital, Medical officers and Corps men to care for them, Medical officers and Corps men to go to Bilibid to care for the sick there. All the rest of us to leave. 700 scheduled and to go at 2:00 AM [Monday the 16th], the remaining to follow. The last to leave, the Staff and the odds and ends, were scheduled for Tuesday at 7:00 AM. All heavy baggage as inspected at 1:00. The packs of the 700 due to leave at 2:00 were gone over. A terrible job. I had come here to write a few pages to you as I had arranged to leave these notes with the hospital to be sent to you upon recapture. I remembered something I had to do and delayed my writing and before I returned, word came from the Japanese headquarters – all outgoing details cancelled. What it means, we can only guess. But we are still here. Three hours later: Change. 190 Field and Company officers to leave at 6:00 AM, the 16th. Not me.

October 16

Very little sleep. I've taken command of Division #1. Its C.O. left this morning. Most of my friends left this morning and there are 250 called for tomorrow at 5:30 AM. The baggage was suspected at 1:30 today. News is good. I still believe that we may never leave for Japan. Our planes were over again today.

October 17

Detail left, but late. At about 7:00 to 7:30 AM our planes appeared again. This time, we could see them quite plainly – about 35 single engine bombers escorted by fighters. Beautiful formation, absolutely no opposition. We saw several such flights, one of which swung north and east and bombed some target on the road between us and the mountains which border on the sea. A group of taff officers came into camp this morning, followed by a truck [6 x2] with guards. They went to the nearby airfield. Quite a lot of troop movement on the road by camp considering that it only goes to a small bay west of here. I expect to leave for Manila Friday or Saturday. But if these attacks continue, I still believe that we will not be sent to Japan. A detail of 250 scheduled to leave at 6:00 AM, another rising 4:00 AM.

October 18

Detail left as per schedule. I was up at 4:00 AM. Our boys were all over again today. Before the detail left they started coming from the cloud bank covering the mountains to the east. From then on, all day long the air vibrated with the roar of their motors, interspersed with detonation of bombs. It is by far the heaviest raid so far. Even the little field close by and was both strafed and bombed, the latter this PM when I was asleep. Our hopes are high. Another letter, dearest, and one from Bill S. I love you so – you are so brave, so fine.

The Colonel's Way

Our planes are over now.
Cabanatuan, P.I.
Thursday, October 19

My darling Judy,

    Our days are about to come to a close. Our last detail that was scheduled to leave tomorrow was called and left at 10:30 AM. There are but 93 of us left and I suppose we will go tomorrow. This will leave 401 patients, eight doctors and some Medical Corps E.M., in the hospital, 16 disabled officers and about 200 disabled soldiers, sailors and civilians, plus 17 well men to run the light plant, pumps, trucks, etc. All of those who have left in the past two weeks are in Bilibid enroute to Japan. But, as it appears that a general attack is on, I doubt if they or we will ever leave.

    Please, above all, do not worry about me. My health all through has been excellent, no malaria, no dysentery. At present, I am a little thin but have been putting on weight for the last three weeks. From now on out, if it is in Bilibid or to Japan, the food is going to be very thin. But I have quite enough vitamins to get by okay.

    As to my financial status, all of my pay is due from December 1, 1941, less my allotment to you and insurance, and half a ration [soldiers] per day from January 1, 1942 to April 9, 1942. Pay from the Japs has been in Occupation Script which has no value. I have given checks in camp four [4] at $200 each. Please see that they are covered as they may be cleared from here before I get home. This record is first for you and secondly to refresh my memory in case I am called upon to testify after the war. So be careful to whom you tell its contents either wholly or in part except the propaganda which I have enclosed.

    About the place, I know you've done wonders, but in planning for the future there are some things that should be put in this spring for they will take a year or so before they bear, asparagus and the berries [raspberries,etc.] I thought they could be north of the house and west of the old orchard. I've enclosed some sketches for you.

    Give each of our grand lads a big hug and kiss for me. Tell them about my going here and that I will be home soon. I live only for the days that are to come when I can hold you in my arms again and tell you how much I love you. I believe as soon as the war is over we can see our way to go right to 'Our Decision' and stay, sending the boys to the high school at Alexandria and then to college at Maryland or Johns Hopkins. Until those happy days, my dearest Judy mine, 'Au Revoir'.

                              I love you, Arthur

The Colonel's Way

DIARY FOUR

{October 23, 1944- August 10, 1945}

The Colonel's Way

The Colonel's Way

                                    Bilibid Prison
                                    Manila P.I.

My darling Judy,

I am enclosing a short set of notes that I have kept during my incarceration at the above mentioned hotel for American POWs. I expect our forces now on Philippine soil south of us to be in here soon and these will be sent directly to you. I left at Camp #1, Cabanatuan, P.I., in keeping of Major Emil P. Reed, M.C., whom the Japs left in command of the hospital there, 3 notebooks addressed to you which should reach you in due time. If they do not, write to Reed through the War Department; also Major Steven Sitter, M.C., who was in the hospital there and promised to check on the notes. Upon receipt of them, if anything should have happen to me, you should offer them to the War Department to extract such parts as they want, as some of it, I believe is the sole record. I will be in Japan when this reaches you, waiting for the end which will only be a matter of months. As you will see by reading the enclosed, the Japs have given us some woolens and I have a fine sweater and gloves, so will be OK. Please do not work too hard at Our Decision just because I'm not there to look after you. I will be along shortly and we will go there to stay as soon as we get it fixed to our liking. Give our lads a big hug from their dad, and with all my love for you, my dearest Judy mine,

                                    Yours, Arthur
                                    Bilibid Prison
                                    Manila, P.I.

<u>October 23, 1944</u>

My darling, I have been here since the afternoon of the 21st when we arrived from Cabanatuan. That day we were up at 4:00 AM and left in trucks for here about 140 kilometers away at 7:30 AM. It was the first time I been out of the compound since my arrival, June 4, 1942. All during the trip, which was very uncomfortable and hot in an overcrowded truck [the railroad is out], I was impressed by the rundown, dilapidated look of everything; roads terrible, buildings falling down, no motor transportation except Japanese Army, most of the people in rags, nothing in the markets except local produce, and little of that. I thought there was very little Jap Army and evidence, a few tanks, scattered small convoys of men going both north and south. One thing I will never forget was the large push- carts with three wheels, loaded with all sorts of freight, being pushed by natives. It appeared to me that they are the accepted means of transport since the Japs took over. Upon our arrival, we were fed rice and quartered on the sidewalk beside one of the buildings. I was lucky to have been able to sneak out a mosquito net as they are terrible here. Colonel Johnson and I shared it the first night. On the morning of the 22nd, we moved here, Building #1, an old dormitory with concrete floors on which we sleep 149 officers; two meals a day of rice with sometimes some vegetables or a little meat. I finally found Captain Charles Wyatt whose mother told me to be sure to look him up. He is in the hospital here, quite sick. There are about 1,500 of us here awaiting transportation to Japan, but I feel we will not go as our troops are firmly entrenched in the central islands.

October 24

And we were awakened by an air raid alert before dawn; fed rice and had just started to eat, when our planes came. The Jap alarm is very poor; our first bombs had hit before the siren blew. We were all chased inside and will probably stay all day. The raid was not heavy but they may come again as it is only 8:45 AM, but it makes us feel better. There is one toilet for all of us inside; a bit crowded. The all clear sounded just before noon, followed by two more in the PM, though we did not see any planes or hear any bombs.

October 25

Three years today since I say good-bye to you, my darling; a long time but the end is in sight. We have faith, dearest, and I know it will be soon that we will be united. Air raids twice this morning but we did not see any planes or hear bombs. Rumors are strong that we landed on Luzon last night; there were lots of Jap planes up from midnight on last night. Our second meal here is plain rice.

October 27

Four wonderful letters. You get a lot in 25 words. # 50 is your last to arrive. I've received 32 from you so far. We are still under air alert. Alert every day but have not seen any of our planes since the 24th. The Japs leave early in theirs each morning and return late each evening. They are coming in now; it is 5:30 PM. I am terribly proud of our boys; Sandy in junior high – I can hardly believe it. You are doing so much at Our Decision, it will surely be lovely when I get back. Still no word of leaving for Japan; I will feel better when we see more air action.

October 29

Sunday. "I feel better" just as I had filled my mess kit with the delicious 'Lugao' furnished by our hosts, someone said, "Here they are", and the first bombs landed; then the air raid alarm sounded. The bombing lasted about 1 ¾ hours; we are still under alert but our planes have gone. Some of my friends who live in one of the two-story buildings said we lost two planes, bombed the air fields, port area, covered the Bay and strafed the boulevard. Our trip is, I hope, delayed again. Life here is quite simple; food our principle concern. I have traded around and gotten some sugar and mongo beans, and hope to get more. We are to be paid today, I hear, and then are to be allowed to purchase some coconuts, tobacco and garlic. Also we are to start a General Mess Fund with contributions from our Postal Savings. Johnson and I continue to sleep under one mosquito bar, and as it is almost impossible to keep all mosquitoes out, we wear long trousers, socks on hands and feet and shirts on. The remarkable thing is that I sleep quite well. Yesterday we were questioned as to our middle name, duty at the time of surrender, and occupation other than soldiering. The Japs must think us queer as no Regular could do anything but soldier. Two more heavy raids; one at 12:50 AM and one at 4:00 PM. Pay day has been put off; I suppose too much air activity.

November 1

Still here. We were given a medical check yesterday consisting of a rectal smear. I understand it will show typhoid carriers, bacillary dysentery and other communicable diseases. All perfunctory; I believe no one will be taken off the lists. No air activity for three days. I hope our planes will be over tomorrow. What little food I was able to bring is gone. One gets terribly hunger on two meals such as we get.

November 3

Friday. Yesterday we were in issued a woolen uniform [Jap soldier]. You can imagine how a group of American officers look in secondhand Japanese uniforms. Lots of wisecracks; all of the sleeves are too short and the hips too big. I put mine under my blanket to add to my padding; I have yet to try it on. Our whole baggage was released to us; we were told that it would be turned in 24 hours before we go on the boat. No air raids since Sunday. If they do not come today I am out a bottle of scotch whisky on a bet. Some of our lads are becoming discouraged; not me. I still feel that we are not going to Japan. Dreams of you, my dearest, so real. Good omen.

November 5

Sunday. Just at breakfast time we heard the welcome sound of our motors and sure enough, before I was served or the raid alarm was sounded, the first bomb hit. Of course, we were sent inside, but not fast enough to suit the Japs who threw stones at us to hurry us on our way. The objectives seem to be quite distant as the detonations were not very clear. A 9:45 they were back again; this time I happened to see them long before the alarm went. They came in a high from the northeast. I did not have time to count them but there must have been nearly 100 bombers and fighters. The all clear just went; it is 10:45. I had a bad day, stomach upset, but I am okay today. My, but the food is bad; soft cooked rice to just fill your mess kit for breakfast; and 3:00 PM the same rice with a little ground corn or sometimes a few beans and some soup made of the native camote with a little coconut oil which, when served looks for all the world like blue-gray garbage water. The camotes are not peeled to avoid waste. Three times we have had a mess spoonful of dried fish about 1 ½ inches long which are eaten, insides, head and all. 12:10, two big events: just as I opened a letter, your #9, March 19, 1943, some yank in a fighter opened up with this MG's and so another raid is on. We certainly gave them a lacing this time. Your letter was, though old, a great joy; nice to get a long one. You are so brave and I love you so. 2:30 PM. Our boys are back again; we have been inside since 9:45 AM.

November 7

We were awakened at 4:30 AM yesterday by the air raid alarm. I thought at first that the Japs had made a mistake but in a few minutes we heard the bombs hit and some strafing; then I went back to sleep. At 7:15 they were back again, and again at 12:30, the latter very heavy with lots of AA. No report of any of our planes being hit. I can see a small piece of the sky through the bars. I saw 25 to 30 dive out of the clouds, right through the AA to unload and strafe; beautiful sight. Several of the buildings have been hit with fragments. One of our officers nearly carried as his epitaph, "killed in the can"; as an explosive bullet came through the roof of the bathroom and knocked a hole in the floor while he was in there. Our news services beginning to function; things look good. I'm still a little upset.

November 8

News has come in that we sank five transports in Manila Bay, sank one cruiser and damaged one other; also at Subic Bay- sank five transports, two subs, one destroyer and damage one other; shot down 91 planes and destroyed 104 on the fields. I am sure we had a ticket on one of those boats. The report was as of Sunday. This [12:30] is the bad time of day; our second meal is not until 3:00 or 3:30 PM, but by now we are all weak from hunger. Our knees shake and if you have to move, it is done at slow motion. Drinking a little water with a few grains of salt helps some. Our ration of 300 g of rice and corn is always short. For the last two days it has averaged 251 g with our few vegetables and 25 g of fish twice a week, we get from 1000 of 1500 calories a day representing from 10 to 15 thin slices of bread. I am still upset; will go to sick call at 5:00 PM.

November 10

Typhoon began yesterday and grew in intensity all day, reaching its peak, I think last night when even in here behind these walls, the wind blew until I thought the roof was going to leave us. I had a bad day; most of picked up some bacillary dysentery. The doctor put me on sulfur – grenadine and although I feel better the sulfur always makes one feel rough. Last night around 5:30 there were some shots fired which were immediately followed by MG bursts. We were all sent inside and the firing continued, both rifle and MG. Lots of Japs came into the compound and for time there was considerable excitement. Rumor has it that some Filipinos tried to escape and that's six were shot. Another rumor is that the guards were being sniped at from the city; both are rumors. I feel the latter is more probable as some of the bullets came over here. The typhoon is abating; we are under air alert.

November 12

Went to church this morning but found even that pretty strenuous on this ration. I wonder what you and our lads are doing; the boys, I suppose, have gone to a movie or you are all at Our Decision. I pray that you are not worrying about me. I am doing okay, expect to contain you do so. My trouble is all cleared up; all I need is a little food and you. Everybody is out of tobacco and I am no exception, so I have stopped smoking. I lost a bottle of whiskey; the bombers did not come over today. I was even, up till now.

November 13

I am even again as I bet that our boys would come over today and at about 7:45 AM they arrived; it is now about 11:00 AM. They have practically been all over this area constantly as at no time since the raid has the sound of their motors not been quite audible. By far, the most constant, if not the heaviest raid. We believe that there must be some naval vessels in the bay. It is cool enough now, early in the morning, to have to use a blanket; the days are always hot in Manila. More later. 4:05; the release from raid has just gone; we are still under alert. For more than 8 hours our planes were constantly over. There goes the alarm again, 4:28. We have had no food and will get none until the raid is over. The Japs are very nervous, throwing rocks and slapping people caught looking out the windows that have no covers that can be closed. We were finally fed at around 5:00 PM and the raid alarm was released at 7:30 PM; the alert continues. Just as soon as we were allowed to go out [about 5:00 PM] everyone took advantage of the chance to get some fresh air and wash and clean mess gear. Great fires were burning along the entire length of the waterfront and it many other points in the city. The Japanese had reinforced their sentries within the compound and also issued orders that all shell fragments, MG links and slugs falling in the prison be turned into them. All are ready for bed. Long day when locked in; no food; we like it?

November 14

We were under alert all night, so consequently were gotten up before daylight to be counted and fed rice just as it got light. This time the Japs knew what they were doing. A few fighters [we counted 13] took the air, and at 8:05 our planes arrived. We could hear some air fighting and then came the dive bombers back to the

The Colonel's Way

harbor and port area. Fires again; that area must be in shambles. Raids close by, but now in Manila, continue. It is now 8:55 AM. Not 5 minutes have transpired and the raid is over Manila again; lots of diving and strafing. 10:45, released from raid to alert. We're held in until 4:10 PM when the local [Bilibid] 'all clear' for raid was given and we were fed fish soup with greens and rice. One short alarm was sounded after we finished eating and we remained on alert all night.

November 15

Up before dawn; still under alert. 153 indigent left in two echelons, destination rumored to be Fort McKinley. With them are doctors, Corps men, chaplain, tailor, etc. Enough to make about 170. I have wagered one whiskey our boys will be over to day; no sign yet, but it is early, 8:00 AM. Well, I guess I lost my bet; none of our planes today. Manila went on all clear at about 4:00 PM.

November 17

Not much in the way of news. One of our truck drivers on duty at Cabanatuan came in. He had been part of a convoy which brought the first of about 250 indigents and Medical Corps men to Fort McKinley. The airfield near our old camp had been hit early on Wednesday [15th]. Short alert near noon.

November 18

Japanese fighters patrolling over Manila, started at about 7:30; they must be expecting. Patrol flew all morning but no Americans appeared. Spend most of the day reading, *Look to the Mountain*; I enjoyed it. Supper, late: 5:00 PM; long time between meals. I'm

The Colonel's Way

surprised how little I miss tobacco; four days now since I stopped smoking, refusing now offers of a cigarettes or pipe-full. At first I thought I would get hungrier than usual but I am coming to the belief that if food is 'few and far between' you do better without. Our nights are full of strange sounds, now and then an explosion, rifle or MG fire, whistles, planes. We are in complete ignorance of the local situation. Our world news is excellent.

<ins>November 19</ins>

Awakened at 5:50 AM by raid alarm. At 7:00 AM we were counted, put back in and fed. At about 8:10 we had a light attack, I believe by high level bombers. We heard some aerial combat firing, some AA, heard some bombs but saw no planes. Low to medium overcast. It is now about 9:30; no planes in evidence. 11:15 AM; another raid, not very heavy, but they are still overhead. Inside of Bilibid there it is a separate alarm system; the city siren blows, then the guard rings a bell. When the guard or O. D. thinks it's clear, he rings the bell and we can go out of the building. I just came by the guardhouse; planes could be plainly heard but above the overcast. The Japs were trying to make up their minds as to who it was when the bombs hit. I can hear the rumble of our motors. 1:50 PM; back again, heavier than the previous one. Through the bars we caught a glimpse of some dive bombers working the port area and the bay. Bilibid; all clear at about 5:15 PM. No shave, no bath, glad to be able to wash mess gear. Good day. Johnson and I bought a kilo of sugar on the black market, $15.00 American; some price! Still under alert, we go to bed.

The Colonel's Way

November 20

Three years today I arrived in the Philippines. Too long. Three days is too long without you. Late last night 70 men arrived from Cabanatuan enroute to McKinley. I had a brief talk with Sgt. Mitchell and Jack Fogleman who used to take care of us at Camp #1. They spoke of seeing a heavy attack on the field near #1 and planes in the air all during the trip down. There are 511 left a Cabanatuan. No raid today. I'm currently reading; *Life of Francis Drake* and *The Raven*; [Sam Houston]. Our food has improved slightly; nearly every morning we have coconut in our lugao and fish with coconut another meal [25 to 35 g].

November 21

Awakened at 4:25 by raid alarm. During the morning the November payroll was brought around and we signed; we have yet to be paid for October. From raid alarm to alert at about 12:00 PM. No sign of planes. Lunch / supper, late 4:30 PM; we have some fried cassava root; a treat.

November 22

Up at 6:00 AM in the dark; still under alert but no planes. Finally, at about noon, the all clear came. We have been fortunate in the food we have been getting; rice with corn, cassava, greens soup, and a small portion of dried fish and coconut. It has made our meal late but we will gladly wait.

November 24

Our diet is back to rice and corn twice a day and you can really feel the difference. Mail from home; I did not hit yet; hope mine will be in tomorrows.

November 25

Air raid alarm while breakfast was being served. The Japs were already up. I cannot tell if our boys have arrived yet, too much local noise, although I believe that I hear combat MG fire and planes diving. More later, it is just 8:00 AM. There goes the A.A., and then the detonation of the bombs; appears to be in the port area and harbor. 8:15 AM. Quite a heavy raid; Bilibid only, all-clear at 9:10 AM. Just stepped out to wash my mess gear when a single shipboard fighter came over and about 4,000 feet. It was a plain to us that it was one of ours but it was not to our stupid guards who looked and smiled until the AA opened up, then there was ringing of bells and much shouting and pushing to get us inside again. No relief until after we had been allowed to send four officers for our rice which we got at 3:30 PM. At about five we were given Bilibid all-clear at 5:30 the Manila alarm sounded the alert, and we got about ¼ cup of fish soup. And so to bed at 8:00 PM, under alert.

November 26

Up in the dark to be counted and stood there for all over ½ hour waiting for the Nippon sergeant. To illustrate the fine sportsmanship of the Japs, yesterday during the raid a plane was shot down; the Japs sentries in and around our kitchen gestured and smiled believing it to be an American plane. When it got low enough to be identified it turned out to be a Japanese plane, whereupon our men were slapped and knocked around with the rice paddles. Such a vivid dream of you, my Judy, back in the house in Dayton. Nana was there; we were going out but I stopped you in the lower hall just to tell you how much I loved you. Lunch / supper is here, rice and fish.

November 27

No alarm. Late yesterday three Jap bombers came over towing gliders, the first I have seen. Manila prices: rice -12,000 pesos, sugar-6000 pesos, mongo beans-8000 pesos, bananas-1:50 to 7 pesos depending on size.

November 28

We have at long last been paid. Major Wilson, MD., the nominal commander here, after consulting the barracks commanders and some of our senior officers, decided to pool all of the officers' pay, amounting to approximately 88,000 pesos, to which was added 56,000 pesos of Welfare deducted from Postal Savings, and placed it in the Commissary to be used as follows: purchase if possible; one package of tobacco per man, some garlic and some salt and issue these to each and all; the remainder to be spent for food for the General mess. This has to be done. We were issued today one package of cigarettes, native [30]. ½ canteen cup of salt and five bulbs of garlic. Some coconuts have been delivered to the mess along with seven sacks of mongo beans at 7,600 pesos per sack. I will note later the total purchase. One thing that influenced the decision was that the total payroll was given to headquarters in 100 peso and 10 peso bills; no way to make change. A wise decision.

November 30

Thanksgiving. By the grace of God, I have much to be thankful for. I have my Judy and our lads waiting for me in the grandest, greatest country in the world, I am all in one piece, in fair health, and I am still eating, though not much. I am still in the Philippine islands and believe I have a good chance of staying. Air alert just after breakfast but no planes as yet. I have a bet up on tomorrow that we will be in. Yesterday, all who did not have mosquito nets were issued squad nets [10 men]. A good sign; news is good.

December 1

Darling, just after I finished my entry yesterday I received 14 letters of which eight were from you, one from cousin Fanny, one Bill, one Rosalie, three mother. Oh, my darling! Words cannot express my feelings, so mixed with pride and love. I am not at all ashamed of the tears that came into my eyes as I read your first letters to me, of the months on end when I had disappeared into the blue as it were, and you had no idea if I was still in the land of the living. So many questions have been answered that I longed to know. You've done a wonderful job, my Judy. I still worry about you working too hard for I know so well your enthusiasm once you get started. You are certainly a successful gardener and will put my little experience to shame when I get back. You can show me and I will do the work, as it should be. The boys, I know, are just as I would wish them. I am so glad they have been such a help. Long pants on both of them! I can hardly believe it. Speaking of your sylph-like a figure, you should see mine after these many months on little or no food. I have read all of your letters three times and have just put them in with the others. I have received 40 from you to date, very good. I am thankful. No raid today.

December 4

Our planes are conspicuous by their absence, but it causes us no worry for we have been practically told by the local Japs that we are not scheduled to go to Japan. Little or nothing has gone on; our food is getting no better fast; greens and rice, some fish but little, and we all continue to get thinner. I was able to get through the Commissary and charge to my Postal Savings, 3 yards of cheap cloth, light salmon in color, at the bargain price of $6.80 pesos per yard. I am busy on a shirt or jacket. I hope to get it home with me. Speaking of Postal Savings, we haven't seen ours for months. In Japan, everyone has what is called a 'chop', or stamp, with his surname on it which he uses on all legal papers in lieu of a signature. The Japs have our chops so heaven only knows what our accounts are. We care less. I think of you every hour of the day, dearest; dreams of our future together, so many things for us to have such fun together, our lads, our lovely place.

December 6

Due, I suppose, to our aerial activity, we cannot start up breakfast rice until 3:00 AM, which is not enough time to prepare for 2,200 men and serve it by 6:00 AM so we get it half done. I have developed the common ailment of swollen legs due to several causes; lack of vitamins in protein deficiency, etc. I am receiving extra B-1 and Colonel North has arranged for some plasma shots for me. I have nearly finished my jacket. It is very fetching. I had my blood plasma, 500 CC's. I had quite a good reaction and have lost a lot of liquid since this morning. I am to get another shot on the eighth.

December 8

Three years ago today: **war!** It hardly seems possible that I could have existed so long without my love. Looking back, it seems time without end, but it must end and I believe soon. When we are united it will seem like a bad dream. I receive my second shot of blood plasma; too early yet to see the reaction. I have had little or no swelling in the legs since my first shot. No air activity for 13 days; I expect some before the 10th or 12th. One of our Naval officers, Scott from Philadelphia, was picked up by the Japs for giving a talk on wines; he was later released. The Japs are very nervous.

December 12

We have had a short period of rain, I hope ended, as it was clear most of yesterday. We have received a soap issue of ½ small box of washing powder, the kind that is used for scrubbing and in washing machines; I am sure it will do well on the complexion. My swelling seems to be under control; hope that I can keep it there. We have rumors that the Japs have had to discontinue the air raid alarms do to misbehavior of the Filipinos, looting, sabotage, etc. This is borne out by a report that a cruiser was damaged in the Bay about four days ago and we had no alarm. It is still overcast; we hope for air action. It makes us feel more secure. Good news from Europe. Later: great to-do. The Japs are preparing us for departure again. The fact that we are going, of course, is not established. We went through before one of our own doctors this AM, check, I suppose, on those able to walk and those who have to be trucked. Of course, none of us want to go to Japan but the real tragedy is our poor condition. We have lost so much weight and condition, that the trip, which will be made in the hold of a ship with no place to bathe and no more food, all this with the change to cold winter after three years in the tropics, will take a toll in lives. I am fortunate to have escaped the infectious diseases so I am and fair shape if they can get us out.

December 13

The detail of 1,619 officers, men and civilians was assembled early this morning with their equipment. Our destination was plainly Japan. Each officer had been issued the Japanese soldiers' secondhand woolen uniform and no provision has been made for

The Colonel's Way

head covering, socks, or foot wear. All members of the detail had been issued soap and two packages of Japanese cigarettes. The details fell in at about 8:30 AM. After being checked, was told of fallout and await further orders. About 11:30 AM the word was passed around to reform the detail. We were marched out of Bilibid Prison, through downtown Manila towards the port area. Colonel Warner, from Baltimore, who had not been well, suffered severely from a combination of the heat and physical fatigue and finally stumbled and fell. An effort was made to place him on a truck driven by a Japanese soldier, but the officer in charge did not allow it. Some of his fellow officers finally assisted him and he made the march successfully to Pier 20. Lying beside was a very nice looking modern vessel about 10,000 tons displaced, called the Oryoku Maru. At about 2:00 PM we were loaded into the vessel which turned out to be one of the so-called Japanese luxury liners, which had made the Manila run before the war. The holds in which we were placed were really trunk compartments and no means of ventilation or lighting was provided. The forward hold into which Colonel Warner and myself and many other officers were placed had been loaded with hay and there were some remnants of it's still in the hold. I imagine that over 500 men were packed in with us and it made it so crowded that no one had sufficient room to lie down. There was only the barest place to sit with your knees drawn up on your chin. Protestations were made to the Japanese about the overcrowding and we were told that readjustments would be made at some later time. An evening meal of rice and fish with a small amount of water was served. Very shortly after dark the vessel got underway. Absolutely no ventilation was provided. The air became very foul. Colonel Brettell and Colonel Conety, who both suffer from asthma, were soon in critical condition. After long protestations to the Japanese we were finally allowed to send them up the ladder to the deck, but for some reason which I will never know, we were soon made to bring them back again. Both died that night. In addition, I estimate over 25 men died in the forward hold that night from suffocation.

December 14

At about 7:00 AM a meal was served which corresponded to the evening meal before. The ration of water was particularly short. The men who went on deck to receive the food reported that we were traveling in a heavily armed convoy and were probably off the west coast of Luzon. At around 8:30 AM we suffered a violent air attack which consisted of dive bombing and very heavy strafing from our Naval Air Forces. These attacks continued with increasing intensity until about 4:30 that afternoon. From what we could hear and feel, the vessel had been severely hit. One bomb had landed on the deck above the hold in which we were placed and had blown one of the three anti-aircraft guns, [which were on deck immediately forward of the hatch which led to the hold], over the side into the ocean. The casualties among the gun crews have been terrible, as also among the passengers who were crowded into every available space in the boat. Later that afternoon during, I believe, the last attack, direct machine gun fire from our planes came through the open hatch severely wounding many of our men. While assisting Colonel North, one of our Medical officers, in the care of the wounded, I received a machine gun wound in the back. Not bad, for I did not realize that I had been hit until someone called my attention to it. Just after dark our Medical officer was sent for, evidently to assist in caring for the Japanese who had been killed and wounded during the attack. Colonel North, upon his return, described the conditions on deck as being a horrible. Casualties of men, women and children were strewn about the deck. The vessel was on fire and had evidently dropped out of the convoy. During the night we could hear the winches running furiously and we assumed that the Japanese are taking off any survivors. We received neither food nor water that night. The heat was so terrific that everyone still alive was constantly in a violent perspiration. This so irritated the men's eyes that they became practically blind. I know, for this happened to me. Sometime during the night of the December 14-15th, Colonel North later told me that I had been overcome by heat and exhaustion and that he had to administer morphine in an effort to save my life. While under the influence, I'd evidently wandered off, for I remember falling from a wooden shelf which is about 4 ½ feet high, which divided the hold into two levels. Someone moved me back up. During this period many of our men became insane. Some attempted to leave the hold and were shot by the guards. There were about 100 casualties from suffocation alone.

December 15

Shortly after daybreak we were notified by the Japanese that we would be permitted to abandon the ship but we were also told that we would not be allowed to take but the barest necessities; mess kit, canteen, shoes and what little other clothing we had. We were told that anyone carrying too much would indicate their intention to try and escape and they would be immediately shot. I estimate that about 9:30 or 10:00 we were allowed to abandon ship. No life preservers or boats were provided. Primarily, my equipment consisted of a pair of shorts, a pair of shoes which I tied around my neck, a pistol belt with a canteen and a mess kit. I picked up an old towel and tied it around my neck with a thought of having protection from the sun. I could find none of my belongings in the terrible disorder in the hold. When I finally reached the deck, the

The Colonel's Way

air was so fresh in comparison to the hold that you were really overcome simply by the amount of oxygen which you could take into your lungs. Several of the men fainted when they first came out into the fresh air. Colonel North's description was certainly true, the vessel was in shambles. I was quite surprised to see large quantities of containers such as the tin powdered milk and the corned beef, butter and other containers of Red Cross food packages destined for prisoners of war, strewn over the decks. The Japanese herded us over the side. I held my nose and stepped off, I imagine about 55 feet high. My impact with the water was so great that my pistol belt became unhooked and I lost the canteen and my mess kit. The cool water of Subic Bay instantly revived us and after looking the situation over with an idea of escape, I finally decided that it was too risky. I struck out for shore, about a quarter to a third of a mile away. When the water became shallow enough for me to stand, I looked back and decided that it might be a good idea if I swam back in an effort to get a canteen and mess kit. I also noticed that there were men still standing on the vessel although she was still burning furiously. The thought occurred to me that in all possibility these men did not know how to swim. I collected up a piece of hatch cover and used it as the Hawaiians do as a surfboard, and paddled back to the vessel, I called up and inquired who couldn't swim and told them that if they would get overboard, I would support them until they could to get the hatch cover which I brought back with me. I instructed one of the officers who I know to bring a belt, canteen and mess kit with him, which he did. As each man jumped overboard I assisted him to the hatch cover and told two to hold on to each side. I then held on to the rear of the hatch cover and pushed the four of them ashore. One of them was Hendrickson, a field artillery man, who was later lost. The Japanese had placed machine guns along the shore and anyone who didn't come directly from the ship to the shore was immediately taken under fire. I know that several of our officers and men were killed that way. As we came ashore we were herded by the Japanese guards back from the beach and finally under a large group of trees which was next to a small garden which had once been part of our naval base. Fortunately, there was a water spigot available and after much protestations, the Japanese allowed us to fill our canteens, the first water that some of us had had for nearly two days. During this time our naval planes came again and, as there was no resistance from the ship, they dropped several bombs which broke her in two and she sank. I found out from some of my acquaintances that the ship actually contained three of these so-called holds or trunk compartments and that a few of them had been placed in the center one. The majority, however, like myself, had been placed in either the forward or the after hold. The center hold had very few officers and men in it. They didn't suffer at all from lack of water and air and were very comfortable, having been able to lie down to sleep. Those in the after hold had suffer severely in casualties and wounds from a near miss which landed close to the stern of the vessel, caving in the plates and causing the deck to collapse above them. We estimated that between 125 and 150 were killed. Later that afternoon we were herded into a single tennis court which fortunately had a spigot in it so we didn't suffer from lack of water. We had had no food since the previous morning. The Japanese made no attempt to feed us. Very few of the men had any clothes. Many had been wounded. The Japanese made no attempt to relieve this situation. One of our men, a marine corporal, had had his arm broken during the bombing. It became necessary to amputate, which was done by one of our medical officers, Colonel Schwartz, with the aid of a razor blade. Repeated entreaties for food and clothing fell on deaf ears. Just before dark an effort was made to ascertain the number of men who survived. A rough count revealed that 1,341 of the original 1,619 were on the tennis court.

December 20

We have now been on the tennis court for five days. During this time, we have been issued three level mess spoons of uncooked rice per day. Some salvage Japanese under clothing was finally brought and our men most in need received either some old under-drawers or the Japanese cotton issue shirt. At about 12:00 PM orders were received for one half of the group to march out of the tennis court. Babcock, who had been with me, and also Bill North were both in this detail. We were placed on trucks, about 30 men to each truck, and moved directly to San Fernando in the province of Pampanga, where we were placed in the Provincial Prison courtyard. This had a gravel area surrounded by high concrete walls containing a few solitary cells. We were fed that day cooked rice for the first time since the 14th of December. Our sickest and most severely wounded were segregated into one of the cell blocks. We tried to make them as comfortable as possible. Our medical officers were given one box of Red Cross medical supplies, which gave us very meager supply of the barest essentials needed for the care of our wounded. We had no medication for the treatment of diarrhea and dysentery which is very current. As the senior officer present, I assumed command of these men. Engelhart acted as my interpreter. I protested through Engelhart to the senior Japanese officer present, a corporal, that our men needed above all, food, but particularly something more than plain rice. I also requested that I get in touch with the Philippine Relief Agency in town with that effort to get our men some sandals for the barefooted and some clothing for the naked.

December 23

Repeated protests to the Japanese authorities that several men who had been injured during the sinking and some affected with diseases, for which we had no medication, and who would surely die if they were not transferred to a military prison hospital in Manila, resulted in an order that we were to select from our group of seven of the sickest and most severely wounded and they could be transferred to Bilibid. After consultation, seven of the sickest men were selected and transferred. Among them was Edison of the Coast Artillery. We still received two meals of cooked rice daily, brought in by the Japanese in the morning and in the afternoon. We have been told to organize a cooking detail in order to be issued uncooked rice. Colonel Harper of the field artillery died last night. From what we can hear, the Philippines are under constant air attack and although we have seen no planes, from the sound they are land- based bombers.

December 24

The Japanese have lived up to their policy that we will receive uncooked rice. In the last two days we have received, in addition to about a canteen cup of rice twice a day, a few camotes and enough dried fish so that each one of our men received a portion about as large as a 50¢ piece. We are fortunate that there is plenty of water here and although the Japanese prohibit bathing, I find that at night many of our men [including myself] have been able to take a bath. We are still suffering from the effects of our mistreatment aboard the first transport. Many of the tropical ulcers which were induced by the terrific heat and the foul air have become infected. We have little or no bandages, the same goes for medication to cure these ill-looking ulcers. There are rumors of movement in the air.

The Colonel's Way

December 25

We have been reunited with the remainder of the group which we now find was in the Cine Building in San Fernando. Yesterday morning we were lined up in the prison courtyard and marched in a column of fours, after having received a meager meal, to the rail road station in San Fernando. Our boys certainly gave this place a working over. The railway yard is in shambles and many disabled cars and locomotives are in evidence. About noon we were placed on board steel freight cars. 193 men were placed in each car. As this is a small, narrow gauge railroad, there was not room for all of them to be seated at one time. Our sick and wounded were placed on top of the cars in the boiling midday heat and lashed there to keep them from falling off with ropes. The Japs insisted that they would be more comfortable, but I feel that is also an attempt to prevent the train from being bombed or strafed by our men. We should be very thankful for them, for had it not been for the many bullet holes in the car, surely more of our men would have died from suffocation during the awful trip to San Fernando, La Union. Of course, there was no food or water and several times when the train stopped and the Filipinos made an effort to give us food or water, they were chased away by the Japanese guards. After being on the train from about noon on the 24th until 2:00 AM this morning, we were unloaded on the station platform at San Fernando, La Union, where we were allowed to remain until daybreak. We were then marched through the town of San Fernando, out on the outskirts, to a small Philippines schoolhouse where we were fed one rice ball in the morning and one just after dark. We were issued about ¼ of a canteen cup of water per man, and after being what we supposed was settled down for the night, we were gotten up after dark and marched about 3 ½ are 4 miles to the beach where we are to sleep.

December 26

At about 4:00 AM, we were awakened and an issue of rice balls was made. Of the entire detail, I imagine that only 800 men received any food it all. The remainder just didn't get any as there wasn't enough to go around. The Japanese allowed us to bathe and the ocean which was taken advantage of by all concerned. This afternoon, after lying in the boiling sun all day, we were given a small amount of water. Everyone is so thirsty that what little water is given is immediately consumed. What little has been in my canteen is always long gone to some man with a fever before any additional is issued. It is pitiful to see a man in this heat with a high fever without water.

December 27

We were awakened very early this morning, long before daybreak, and marched about ¼ mile to a pier where we were forced to jump about 20 feet into a Japanese landing boat which were riding a heavy swells in the Lingayen Gulf. We were then taken and placed on a Japanese transport, about 1,000 men on one ship, whose name I have not been able to ascertain, and about 250 on another. We were in the center hold, half of us on the upper deck of the hold and the remainder in the lower hold. It wasn't too crowded as the hatch is very large the air is not too bad. Unfortunately, the upper deck on which my detail has been placed, was used for the transportation of horses and the Japanese, in their usual custom, didn't bother or would not allow us to remove any of the refuse which remained in this vessels hold after evidently, a very long trip. The flies are terrible. I will say that shortly after we came aboard, we were fed probably the best food we have had since we left Cabanatuan. Although the quantity is quite small, it is well cooked and seasoned. About 4 ounces of tea or soup is all the liquid we are allowed. We were fed again late in the afternoon immediately after the vessel got underway.

December 31

Rumor has it they we have arrived at Takao in the harbor of Formosa. I am confident that we are going north as it has become much colder and although we are quite crowded, some of the men are beginning to suffer from the cold. We have been and fed quite regularly, although the food has been far from adequate, particularly the liquid contents. In absence of anyone else in the senior grades, who was either not well enough or didn't care to assume the responsibility, I have organized the hold and have endeavored to see that the food and water is properly distributed to all. Dysentery is on the increase, which I understand from our medical authorities is quite common. Never once have the Japanese, even though we protested severely, supplied us with enough buckets to meet our sanitary requirements and, although every effort is made to keep things as clean as possible, the ship is in a very unsanitary condition.

January 5, 1945

It has been definitely establish that we are in the Harbor of Takao in Formosa, and have been since our arrival on the 31st of December. The Japanese are evidently celebrating the New Year for we have seen little or nothing of them in the last five days. Fortunately, we have been able to remove some of the refuse in clean up the hold somewhat. Our food remains about the same. The shortage of liquids is extremely hard on our sick men, and we have had quite a few casualties in the last five days. Colonel Beecher, our senior officer, has not been at all well, and a great deal of the load of the administration of the men, has fallen to me.

The weather has turned quite cool and with our scanty clothing it is very difficult to keep warm. The sanitary conditions still remain quite critical and it is only through constant protestations that the Japanese allow us to empty the refuse daily. If this is not done, the conditions are beyond description.

January 6

A small detail which was loaded on a different vessel when we left the Philippines, has been brought aboard this ship. We now have approximately 1,300 men who are all in this, the second hold, but we are separated on two levels, the count is approximately the same. The food, when it is given to us, is all delivered on this, the upper deck of the hold, where we divide it and send the share of the men in the lower hold down to them. The shortage of containers is very critical. The Japanese demand that we immediately empty the rice and return the container to be filled again. This is extremely difficult, the flies are terrible problem, and we have absolutely no place where the rice can be divided equally among the men. Major Ridgley, of the Marine Corps, is in charge and is doing a wonderful job.

January 8

Thirty-four Dutch and British prisoners were today removed from the ship and about 500 of our people, mostly from the lower level, were moved and placed in the #1, or forward hold, of this vessel. This sounds like a simple operation but, as are men are so weak from exposure and lack of food, it has taken nearly the entire day to accomplish this move. After the men were brought out from the lower hold, the Japanese began to load on unrefined sugar into the lower hold. This has created quite a problem for our men who, of course, are near starvation and cannot resist the temptation to steal the sugar. The Japanese unfortunately saw someone in the lower part of the hold and have told us if the guilty men are not immediately delivered to them, we will receive no more food. This crisis was met by two extremely brave men who volunteered to admit that they had been stealing the sugar. It makes one extremely proud that our men react so well under these horrible conditions. The two men were taken before the Japanese commander, and I will say, got off quite well. They were severely reprimanded and slapped around a little bit, sent below and told not to do it again. We have now become better organized and send one man from each group down in the lower level to get sugar for the people in his immediate group. We are, of course extremely careful to see that they're not discovered.

January 11

On the morning of the 9th at around 9:00 AM, we were again brought under air attack. We had just received, and were in the act of distributing the food for the first meal of the day when the alert sirens were blown and the ship, with the tanker which was lying next to her, were heavily attacked by our Air Force. First with strafing, followed immediately by bombing. The vessel suffered two direct hits astern, immediately followed by direct hit on the corner of the hatch immediately above us, and another one in the vicinity of the hatch in the forward hold. Also, a near miss off the port bow directly abeam of the forward hold. The bomb which landed directly above us blew all of the heavy hatch covering down into the hold and many of our men were killed and injured as a result. I believe that the most disastrous was the near miss just off the port bow, as it blew hundreds of plates not only through the side of the ship, but also through the bulkhead which separated our hold from the forward hold. I was sitting with my back against this

The Colonel's Way

bulkhead when the attack came. Colonel Babcock who was on my right, and Lt. Roberts who was on my left, were hit. Roberts was decapitated and Babcock quite badly wounded in the chest. Further to my right where the medical officers were assembled up against the side of the ship, the casualties were very heavy. Our losses in the second, or mid- ship hold, were in no way as severe as in the forward hold. Through the holes in the bulkhead it was possible for us to look into the forward hold. The carnage was terrific! One side of the ship was quite badly caved in, and the plates making up the floor were severely buckled. In addition, there were hundreds upon hundreds of plates in the ship and fragments which broke off during the bombing, causing tremendous casualties. I estimated that least between 275 and 300 were killed outright, and about 250 wounded. The concussion was so bad that the men who were serving the meal on the hatch which separated the lower and upper levels of the hold in which we were in, were all blown off and dropped about 25 or 30 feet to the floor of the lower hold. Sea water was blown in, in great quantities through the upper hatch. After things quieted down a little, I undertook to trying to clean up as best I could. Capt. Webb, from the Oklahoma Agricultural College, was one of my mainstays. I organized a detail of men who were considerably well and we placed all of the bodies of those who were killed to one side. With no medication, the problem of the wounded was extremely serious. Many died that night. On the morning of the 10th of January, the survivors of the forward hold were brought back into our hold and we were all placed on the upper level. With the casualties which we have suffered, we are certainly now less than 800 men. This morning the Japanese called for detail to remove the bodies of our dead. I have been told by the men who were on it, that the bodies were loaded on a barge, taken to the Japanese cemetery and cremated where the remains were interred. On the afternoon of the

10th, the Japanese Medical authorities came on board. There were no commissioned officers present. The only medication that they provided was a limited supply of gauze and absorbent cotton and a red solution which I took to be mercurochrome. This, of course, was terribly inadequate as many of our men were severely wounded, many had suffered not only fractures but compound fractures. It is still extremely cold, and we are torn with the problem of freezing or getting the Japanese to close the hatch cover which makes the air extremely bad.

January 14

We have been moved from the ship and placed upon another. This ship, I understand from the men who were separated from us when we left the Philippines, this was the one which brought them to Formosa. She is very old, and quite dirty. We have all been placed on the forward part of the vessel in the #2 hold. It is extremely crowded and very dark. Colonel Beecher and myself, and the other senior officers including the medical officers, are just in the rear of the #1 hatch. Behind us and extending past the #2 hatch, and are the conventional wooden platforms which the Japanese have placed in their holds for their men to sleep on. We are so crowded that it is necessary for our men to lie on the hatch covers under the #2 hatch, i.e., the hatch covers leading below decks. It is here where we have put our sickest men and we have organized some volunteers to try to give them what little care we can. We again are faced with a serious problem of sanitation. Colonel Beecher remains still quite sick and I have had to organize the entire force. H.K. Johnson, I have appointed as my executive, and we have broken the hold down into sections with a field officer in charge of each section. We have appointed a commander who is responsible that the rice and what little water we get is equally distributed between the men. We got underway immediately and hope and pray that our trip to Japan will not be too long. We have been told that we will be twice a day. The food so far has consisted of cooked rice with a little bean paste, about a spoonful for each man, and about ¼ cup of water, so-called tea, twice a day.

January 24

We have been underway about 10 days. Evidently the Japanese are extremely worried about the submarine menace for it appears from what we can hear, we are never allowed to go on deck, that the vessel is in convoy during the day and lies through the night in some small harbor in an effort to dodge our submarines. On several occasions the ships guns have been fired and we have heard explosions in the distance. Our casualties have been very severe. Each morning, I would estimate that the bodies of 20 to 30 men are carried and placed on the upper deck. We hold services for those who died each day, that night. Babcock, who is beside me, is very weak and all of us are suffering severely from the cold. Johnson bartered his ring to one of the Japanese guards, and in return we got one of the straw mats which the Japanese are issued to sleep on. By splitting in two we have now enough to cover about four of us at night when it becomes very cold, the wind blowing in the hatch which is just above us. We're also faced with the same problem with reference to sugar, but this time, profiting by our past experience, we are well organized. Certain men are detailed each night to go below and bring up sufficient sugar and to give everyone a good supply for the day. I am sure that this will save the lives of many of our men, for when one is cold, a tablespoon full of raw sugar is a great help. I've been called upon twice to call the roll which is a very difficult task and takes nearly all afternoon. This old boat has sailed with a very severe list. This makes a tremendously uncomfortable to sleep or even to lie down which one must do to keep warm. All of us have developed terrible sores on our sides as we are so thin that where we lie on the steel decks becomes very painful.

January 25

Colonel Babcock died last night. From our meager supply of medicines I had been able to obtain for him some phenol-barbitol, which on several occasions had made him restless during the night. At about 4:00 AM, he appeared to have become quite restless. I supposed that it was due to either the sedative or the fact that he was getting cold. I attempted to quiet him and pulled the grass mat over him in an attempt to keep him warm. He soon quieted down, but later I realized that he was dead. This was proven by the medical authorities at daybreak. Our ration remains about the same. Sometimes cooked seaweed is substituted for the bean paste. The ration is so small that it makes very little difference. Unfortunately, our water supply seems to be falling off, for although it is issued twice a day the number of buckets that we get are falling off. In addition, the water is frequently quite salty. Protestations to the Japanese have simply resulted in indignities to the officers protesting. It is now quite cold. The upper deck is partially covered with ice and snow and the cold, raw wind, interspersed by snow, greet you when you go on deck. Part of the sanitary facilities which are provided consist of an oblong wooden box which is hung over the side of the ship. It is necessary to climb over the rail and down into the box to use it. This is extremely difficult for our men in a weakened condition. However, a bit of fresh air is worth the risk of falling overboard.

The Colonel's Way

Today, I noticed some Japanese aircraft flying above the convoy. We must be approaching Japan.

January 29

We have arrived, according to the guards, on Moji on the island of Kyushu. This morning we were told that every man must appear on deck for a physical examination. The weather continues very cold. We had great difficulty in getting are sick and weakened men on deck. This was a terrible hardship for us all, for we were required to stand on deck in the freezing weather with practically no clothes, many of our men with no shoes, while we were given a very cursory medical examination by the Japanese. We were told that clothing would be issued in the morning. Late this afternoon, a detail of Japanese women came on board and removed the hatch cover from the deck and also the cover directly below it on the deck where we were quartered and began to unload the sugar that we knew was in the hold below. Many of the sacks, as we knew, were broken and we feared a repercussion from the Japanese; however, none materialized. Great haste was made in unloading the vessel. I imagine from fear of bombing.

January 30

Very early this morning without any food we were told to go to the upper deck and like all Japanese orders, it must be done immediately. Many of our men were so weak and ill that they had to be carried and were unable to stand alone. We were issued some Japanese uniforms but no head coverings. General issue consisted of a pair of long cotton under-drawers, a cotton khaki shirt, a pair of Japanese soldiers' trousers and jacket. No gloves, and in many instances, no footwear was available. Some shoes, of either British or Australian make, and some low-cut Japanese rubber and canvas shoes, were issued. Fortunately, I still retain the pair which I had salvaged from the Oryoku Maru. Immediately afterwards, we were disembarked. This process consisted of marching off of the boat in single file where we were sprayed by a disinfectant all over by a Japanese soldier and then marched to what was apparently an old shed which for some reason contained a theater. Shortly after our arrival there, we were told that some of us would have to return to the vessel to carry those who had been unable to walk. In an effort to inspire them in, I with Colonel Johnson led the first detail back to the vessel. By this time the weather had cleared slightly in the sun shone for a few minutes giving us a welcome warmth, for the shed in which we were quartered had a concrete floor an absolutely no heat. Those who were too ill or too weak to walk were carried back to the shed in pieces of old sacks and laid on the concrete floor. We were then divided into four groups. One, I understand from an interpreter, was to go to a Japanese military hospital, the other three were to be distributed to prison camps on Kyushu. At about 2:30 or 3:00 PM we were given [what I learned from Engelhart] to be what is generally known in Japanese as binto boxes. They consist of two boxes made a very thin wood, one quite small box and the other about the size of our 1 pound candy boxes. In the small box we found small pieces of pickled fish, squab, the conventional salted radishes and other vegetables of which the Japanese are so fond. In the other was, I imagine ¾ pounds of cooked rice which I understand is the normal trips ration in Japan and is usually served in a station where the train stops at mealtime. I will say that, although these boxes were not hot, they were so much better than any of the food our men had in months. A little later Lt. Tachino, who was in charge of our detail, asked for some men to return to the ship to get our breakfast which of course by this time was stone cold. Nevertheless, most of it was eaten in addition to the other meal by our men. Late in the afternoon, three Japanese ambulances, charcoal fueled, arrived and took off our most seriously weak and sick. Just as it became dusk, the detail in which I had fallen, which numbered 193 men, was ordered to assemble in columns of four. We marched through the town about ½ mile, supporting those who were unable to walk, and placed on passenger cars and immediately left the station. The train was lighted and after rather enjoyable ride as the train was heated, we disembarked at a station platform where a tremendous bonfire had been built by a detail of British and Canadian soldiers who had been sent to meet us. The welcome was very warm, particularly as each of us at this time was issued a British or Australian overcoat. One trunk was available to carry us to camp and we sat around the fire and kept warm as it made the several trips necessary to get us into the camp. When my turn arrived we rode for about ½ hour through a blackened out industrial area and arrived at camp, I imagine, around 8:30 or 9:00 PM. For each prisoner there had been delegated by the British senior officer; someone to look after him. I was assisted, or rather, half carried to a long, low building consisting of thin board walls which were dug into the ground about 4 feet leaving about 2 feet of walks exposed above the ground level and a peaked roof covered with tar paper. Inside were the conventional shelves about 6 feet wide covered with matting running the entire length of the building with an aisle of the same width, covered with sand, separating them. Each prisoner was issued 6 blankets, and we were then fed hot tea with sugar in it and soft rice, also was sugar. This was a very invigorating and welcome meal. I immediately rolled up in my six blankets and fell fast asleep.

The Colonel's Way

February 1

We were awakened before daylight and fed hot tea and soft rice porridge and a thin vegetable soup containing soya sauce. I learned from the British soldier in charge that we were in Camp #1 in the Fukuoka District consisting of about 1000 mixed British and Dutch POWs, and that there were about 26 or 28 British officers, the senior- a lieutenant colonel. During this day, our clothes which we had had on board were taken up and we were issued very fine soft woolen OD shirts of British issue and two Japanese uniforms. However, we were only allowed to have one suit of underwear. Just how we are going to wash it is another problem. We also have been ordered two have our heads and faces shaved. A British and NCO within all old fashion razor and cold water performed the operation on me. I must have been a horrible sight when I arrived in camp the night before. Fortunately, there were no mirrors, for some of us would probably die of fright if we could see our condition. It is particularly cold and damp in the home huts and equally as cold outside. But in an effort to break the chill, one of the British non -com's brought in a small metal bucket with holes in which was burning a charcoal fire. His efforts to increase the heat with a green wood only caused a heavy pall of smoke to be collected in the shack. I learned from the British non-com that they get one Red Cross food package to be divided among two people about once a month. There are rumors that we also will receive some Red Cross food.

February 3

We have now been here for nearly four days. Last night we were given an opportunity to take a bath for the first time since leaving the Philippines. I was amazed at the emaciation of not only myself, but all are men. We were literally skin and bone. All of us

The Colonel's Way

without exception are suffering from ulcers which are the result of our trip on the transports. Every man, without exception, has large sores on his hip bones which were occasioned by lying on the steel plates of the vessels. We have been placed in three huts or barracks and so far have not been required to work. There are few, if any, of us who are capable of getting up and getting around. So far, what little has been done for us has been done by the British non- coms. There are two doctors in the camp, one an American and one belonging to the Dutch Army. The tragedy is the lack of medication. There just seems to be none in any of the Japanese camps. I believe that at least ¾ our men are suffering from acute diarrhea which is a result of malnutrition. Several have already contracted pneumonia from the cold. Two have died since we arrived. Last night, just after the evening meal, Colonel Engelhart, one of the officers who is capable of speaking Japanese, came to the door of our barracks and told us that we were to be issued a small amount of Red Cross food. We have been given one Red Cross box from which all the canned meat and fish have been removed. One box was given for three prisoners. When I inquired as to the reason for the removal of the canned meat and fish, I was told that it had been done upon the order of the Camp Commander and that it was customary in this camp for all Red Cross packages to be treated in this manner. Later, according to my informant, we will receive corned beef and the canned salmon as part of the ration issued to us by the Japanese. Our bath is, I believe, common to all Japan; a series of four wooden tubs with concrete floors which are heated from below. Each group or persons is given a certain amount of time. You enter the bath and first wash with soap and water from light wooden buckets, dipping the water out of the large tubs. After you are satisfied with your cleanliness, you are then allowed to get into the large tub and steep in the hot water. Last night was the first time I had been a warm since arriving in

Japan. I can see now why the Japanese think this method of bathing is so good. It is the only way they ever get warm in the winter.

February 7

The NCOs of the British and the Dutch Armies, who have been assisting in the care of our men, have been withdrawn and we have been told that from now on we will have to take care of our own. This puts a very severe strain on our weak and men. We have so many who are unable to care for themselves that the burden which is placed on the remainder, I am afraid, will cause them to become sick themselves. It is necessary that we keep someone on duty during the entire 24 hours as the majority of our men are in such bad condition. We also have been required to wash all the clothes of the men have died and those who are unable to perform this task for themselves. The facilities are practically none. Cold water and no soap. We have also been required to furnish our own food details. It takes about six men to carry the food for each hut; this usually consists of a large wooden box of hot rice with about 40% millet, and a couple of buckets of vegetable soup. We have been furnished two bowls by the Japanese from which to eat. A small one for the soup and a large one for our rice. We have also been informed by the authorities that we can send a message setting forth our safe arrival in Japan. The price is pretty steep; amounting to about $10.00 in American money. It is fortunate that I have a few Filipino pesos which the Japanese have changed to yen, which enables me to send a message home.

February 15

Many changes have taken place since my last entry. The so-called three sick barracks have been broken up. All of us have been

The Colonel's Way

considered well enough by the Japanese doctor and that means those are able to get up and dress themselves have been placed in two barracks at the far end of the camp which recently has been constructed. We have been required to take over the cleaning of this area and of two additional barracks in which the British and Dutch prisoners who are currently disabled are kept. This also includes taking care of the sanitary facilities. As for myself, I have drawn the job of policing the latrines. I have as my assistant a young Air Force officer from Texas. As is the Japanese custom, nothing is provided; the only possible way that we can attain any cleanliness at all is by scrapping the floors of these buildings [there were no seats] with sand, which is abundant, and with that old brick. After this, we sprinkle a light, dry sand in an effort to absorb the moisture which is finally swept out with a broom of our own making, since the Japanese supplied none. There are three of these buildings which serve about 250 men for which we are responsible. Several of the senior officers were called, taken to the small building in which the interpreter lives, and subjected to about a 4 hour questioning by a Japanese Staff officer from the District Headquarters. It is evident by his questioning that news of the treatment which we received in the Philippines has now become world-wide news, for he is very anxious to get our reaction as to how we felt we had been treated. He also seemed to be tremendously interested as to whether it would be possible for us to maintain our supply lines when the final attack upon the Japanese mainland takes place. He even cited as an instance Napoleon's failure to maintain his supply lines during his attack on Russia and his retreat from Moscow. He put the direct question to us; would we say that we would be able to maintain our supply lines if we ever were successful in attacking the Japanese mainland. I should think that the answer is quite evident as our B-29s are daily over this island and I imagine the entire mainland of the Japanese. And it still remains quite cold. It is very difficult for us to get around in our weakened condition with clothes that we must put on to try to keep us warm. The food is still on about the same level. We get something above the usual vegetable soup, I should say, about once or twice a week, a small amount of fish in our soup, or on rare occasions, a boiled squab which is divided between two prisoners. We have inquired as to why, like the other prisoners, we didn't receive any Red Cross food other than the meal we received after our arrival. We have been told that this food had been put aside for the British and Dutch prisoners and that there was none for us. We receive an issue of cigarettes once a week which gives us a total of about three cigarettes a day. I have met and become friendly with a very nice boy from Tacoma, Washington- a civilian who was picked up on Wake Island. He was working for the contractors there when the war broke out. Through him, I am making an effort to obtain some additional money from the British officers, as it is common knowledge that they are well supplied with Japanese yen, having been here for about three years.

February 25

Through the efforts of my friend, Franklin, I've made contact with two British officers from whom I have been able to obtain some funds. The rate of exchange is extremely high as the British demand two American dollars for one Japanese yen. This, of course, is usual. I have obtained a total of 100 yen which has cost me $200. The $50.00 of this I've given to Major Marshall Hurt. We have been able to purchase some of the Japanese B-1 tablets which are simply concentrated yeast tablets, however, the doctor advises us that they are beneficial and we should do everything that we can to preserve our health. There is also available to us

The Colonel's Way

small quantities of bean paste. In my own mind, I sometimes wonder if it is worthwhile to buy these foods on the black market, for I am highly suspicious that both the food and the cigarettes which are available on the black market were stolen by the British who worked in the mess and are sold to us at their own exorbitant prices. We, therefore, simply get a reduction on the amount of food and tobacco issued. We have had one rather major tragedy. A major of the Veterinary Corps and in EM of the Medical Corps were discovered during the morning hours eating a dried squid which they undoubtedly had purchased on the black market. They were immediately taken by the Japanese Commandant where they were very roughly handled. His favorite method of chastisement is to beat around the legs and hips with a heavy bamboo pole. After this treatment they were confined to the Jap guard house or prison. The Japanese are ingenious in making people uncomfortable. The prison consists of small box- like enclosures where it is neither possible to stand up nor to lie down and comfort. In addition, these box-like cells are quite open to the weather and as the men, while incarcerated, are only allowed one blanket, they suffer severely from cold and exposure. They are also allowed only half of our meager ration. Both of these men were confined for four days and were in very bad shape when they were released. The Veterinary officer was suffering from frozen feet, while the Corps man came down in about three days with pneumonia, but he is part Italian from New Mexico and I'm sure that he will pull through. We have been segregated again. Unfortunately, I myself am not feeling too well; I believe the result of over-eating, as I purchased some extra rice from some of the British non-com's. Where they get rice to replace it I don't know. I've been placed in what is known as the 'sick barracks' next to the Sergeant with pneumonia. As senior officer, I am responsible for the barracks. I've been placed on soft rice again. And I'm quite sure that it is easier for me to digest as it doesn't include, as does the normal ration, a large portion of millet, which is hard to digest. The quantity is not as great, but as it only get up once in the morning and once in the afternoon, I believe that I am better off. There are rumors that we, the men in the 'sick barracks', are to receive, instead of rice ration at noon, a small loaf of bread. Several times lately we have been required even at night to leave our huts and go to the air raid shelters. The shelters themselves are extremely crude affairs dug down into the ground about 4 feet and penetrating about 2 feet above ground. They are lined with bamboo and covered with sand. During one of the air raids, I was sitting next to a Dutch boy who was very much concerned that the shelter, due to the concussion of the bombs falling in the nearby city, would collapse. I told him he should have no fear for if the shelter would collapse he would find that he would be then be standing amidst a little broken bamboo and about 6 inches of sand, as the top of the shelters are only covered to that depth. We also have been required to get weighed once a week. This in itself is an ordeal. We go by small groups to the Japanese Medical hut, which like all other huts in this camp is absolutely without heat, where we stand around waiting to be weighed with only our shoes on in the bitter cold. I have gained a very slightly since the last weighing, somewhere in the vicinity of a pound. I now weigh 43 7/10 kilos or a little better than 96 pounds. Some of the British officers who worked in the Japanese headquarters in the nearest town have been able to sneak into camp some Japanese newspapers, so we're not entirely devoid of news. The war in Europe is certainly going well after our setback in the Bulge. As far as this theater is concerned, I am confident that we are doing better than the Japanese admit. From my friends who drop into see me who are in the 'well barracks', I find that the Japanese have made absolutely no difference between the work required by our officers and men. The loveliest and most menial work is performed even by our most senior officers, such as fertilizing the garden, cleaning out the latrines, etc. The hours are quite long, the exact length we are not able to determine, for no one now has a means of recording time. We are awakened before dawn and hold morning roll call as soon as it is light enough for the Japanese to see us. We return immediately to our huts for breakfast and then go to work. There is a short break allowed in the mid- morning where the workers are allowed to go inside the huts sand smoke. Peculiar; here they allow no smoking outside. Everywhere else I've been, they allowed no smoking inside. I believe we get about ½ hour for the noon meal, a short break in mid-afternoon, and it is dark when our men are recalled from work. The evening meal is always after it is quite dark. And the camp is quite heavily blacked out even to the two lights which are left on at night in the huts. Sentries are continually checking to see that black-out instructions are followed. I've just been notified that Marshall Hurt, of whom I am so fond, died yesterday. He was a fine officer. I have his few remaining personal possessions which I will attempt to get back to his next of kin. Our death toll has been quite high. We have lost more than 50 of the original group that arrived in this camp.

March 10

Things continue about the same. I had a visit yesterday from a civilian friend, Franklin, who was picked up by the Japanese on Wake Island. He is recovering from a severe beating with a bamboo pole administered by the Camp Commander. He was suspected of having stolen some Japanese canned rations from a cave where his working party have been storing them, I suppose against our forthcoming attack on Japan. It appears as though Franklin and one of the other prisoners were discovered near a

The Colonel's Way

broken box of rations and although, upon being searched, none were found on him, the Japanese immediately assumed that they had broken into the case and stolen some of the cans. With the usual lack of trial, he was brought up before the Camp Commander and severely beaten around the back and legs with a bamboo pole. The severity of the beating he received can be judged by the fact that he had a cake of Red Cross soap in his hip pocket, which, after the beating, was reduced to a fine powder. He was placed in the Japanese Guard house for three days on half-rations, but as the weather has improved, he fortunately did not suffer from the cold. Of course, he is terribly stiff and sore, but is able to get about. With the advent of warmer weather are death rate has fallen off somewhat. The rations remain about the same. One of the other barracks, in which some of our sickest men have been placed, the ration has been changed so that the men received a small loaf of bread at the noon-day meal. It is not much larger than an ordinary hamburger bun, but it is considerably more in weight due to the fact that the quality of flour is very poor and is heavily diluted with soya bean flour, giving the bread a very dark appearance and making it taste very sour. I have not been at all well and have had to give up working. Evidently the course millet in the rice ration does not agree with me for I find that it produces terrible stomach upsets. The Dutch doctor has recommended that I again be placed on soft rice ration. The camp is now entirely blacked out at night with only one black- out lamp left burning in the center of the barracks. We are constantly being called to the air raid shelter. The B-29 activity is evidently increasing. We have received no further Red Cross food. The cigarette ration has disappeared. I cashed another check for $400 for which I received from the British Sergeant Major 200 yen. One hundred of this I gave to one of our American Medical non-com's who is in pretty bad shape. Our schedule a work remains from dawn until dusk. We work for 13 days and then or allowed one day of rest. There are rumors in the air that we are to be transferred to another camp. Only the officers, including some of the British officers, rumor has it, are to leave.

March 25

Persistent rumors again indicate that we are to be moved to another camp. However, we have received no instructions so far. Considerably more substitute for rice is issued in the ration. In fact, it is hard to find any rice in the rice ration at all.

April 24

Things have changed very little in the last month except possibly for the condition of our men. With the advent of the warmer weather, our sick list has gone down, and although the food has remained practically the same, a general overall improvement seems to be shown. The persistent rumors that we are to be moved have finally materialized. All of the American POWs and 10 of the British officers [senior] have been told that they will leave camp shortly and to be prepared. I was surprised this morning to find out that some of the other officers who had arrived in Japan with us, and had been sent to another camp, were in a barracks at the lower end of this camp. We were prohibited by the Japanese from speaking to them. However, by watching my step, I was able to talk to Wilson and Tarpley, both old friends of mine from the Philippine campaign, who had been in the camp there with me the entire time. They both looked well and from their accounts they have fared better than we. General treatment and the food that they received was much superior to ours.

The Colonel's Way

April 26

We have been told that we will leave can't immediately after lunch today. All of the clothing and the uniform which we have received since we arrived here have to be turned in. We have nothing left except that clothing which was issued as we disembarked at Moji. I am fortunate enough to be able to get a little extra underwear, and Franklin Burns, of whom I spoke previously in this diary, gave me a short woolen jacket. So I am not entirely devoid of clothing. He also gave me an old white hat which is the only thing I have for head cover. However, I am more fortunate than some of my associates, for they have none. I've collected what few articles I have, and placed them in an old Red Cross food carton. These are my sole belongings.

April 30

We have arrived at a new camp in Jinsen, Korea. The trip, for one exception, has been so comfortable and the food has been so good, that I am sure that the Japanese have come to the realization that they are losing the war. We were marched from our camp down the main concrete highway about 3 miles to the town of Fukuoka where we were loaded on a Japanese vessel, which, from all that we can gather [although the Japanese will tell us nothing], is a fast ferry which runs between the islands of Japan and the mainland of Asia. Our group, with that of the British, were placed on board in what we believe are the second class accommodations; a clean, well- kept, large room with the conventional matting on which the Japanese sleep. We were given two of the small wooden boxes containing food and told that that was to be our breakfast as we were supposed to have had our supper before leaving camp. Of course, everyone immediately ate the food. We were just about settled for the night, the lights having been dimmed, when the air alert sounded, and we were hurried off the boat and told to remain on the pier and that we would be told when to get aboard the ship again. According to the usual Japanese custom, we were alerted several times during the night, but it was beginning to get light when we finally were told to get aboard the ship again. It was very cold and we all suffer tremendously. We all finally decided that we were not going to be put on the boat, so we huddled close together on the concrete pier in an effort to keep warm. Upon being re-embarked we were placed in another cabin very similar to the one the night before, not too crowded and with plenty of ventilation, where we all probably went to sleep. I was awakened about noon and told that we would be fed. This time a fish stew and dried rice. Better food than we have ever had before. I was able to go and look out of the porthole. The vessel is quite fast, I estimate about 21 knots, and we are now cruising through a beautiful blue sea with many small rocky islands on the side from which I am looking. At about 4:30 PM, we came alongside of a dock where there was a large railroad terminal, and after some confusion, were unloaded and march to what is evidently a moving picture theater. I saw several of the officers that I had not seen since the early days of captivity. I imagine there are about 200 of us in all. Our group was placed in the balcony, and the Japanese interpreter told the assembled group in the balcony that they would soon be moved to a train, and that those on the first floor it would remain in the theater overnight and leave the following morning. We were again fed the conventional two boxes, one containing dried fish and vegetables and the other good quantity of rice. About 8:00 PM, we were assembled and marched to the railroad terminal about two blocks away, where, much to my surprise, we were placed upon very comfortable day coaches; three officers to every two seats. We were told by the interpreter that we would remain on the train all that night and the following day, late, we would arrive at our destination. The cars, of which there are two, are part of a long freight train which is filled with Japanese soldiers, resembling our passenger coaches in the U.S. They are very comfortable with the usual toilet facilities at each end, spring seats covered with red cloth upholstery. However, the electric system evidently does not work because we have several coal oil lanterns to replace them. The train immediately got underway and we were told to make ourselves comfortable for the night. When I awakened the next morning quite early, we were traveling through a very mountainous section of Asia. After we completed our casual ablutions, the car was cleaned by one of the E. M.'s and at the first station we were given hot tea and the conventional two boxes for breakfast. Having been on such a strict ration for so long, very few of our men are able to eat all of the food. It is carefully put away to be in later. Nothing is wasted. We travelled all that day and were fed both at noon and about 5:00 PM. Tea was also issued. We stopped for about ½ hour at the principle city in Korea, a very modern station built of concrete with individual staircases between two tracks with a platform. Just before dark we arrived at what the Japanese interpreter told us was our final destination and marched through the warehouse section of what is undoubtedly a good- sized city period the interpreter told us that it was Jinsen. We were placed inside of a high compound in which there are large wooden barracks, with stoves and the conventional matting on which we are to sleep. I am impressed by the fact that we have glass windows and they are very clean. Some of the British officers told me that there was a small compliment of British soldiers there who were to take care of us, in addition to our own EM who number about 20. Today we number about 150 officers and 20 EM. The EM have been placed in a barracks of their own, this for the first time. Our senior officers; Majors and Lt. Colonels, in one barracks and our junior officers in another. I

The Colonel's Way

am, as usual, the senior officer, and it is my duty to report to the Japanese twice a day. This has to be done in Japanese. The following morning we were taken into the yard of the compound and after our belongings had been searched, we were addressed by a lieutenant colonel, whose name wasn't given, whom we were told was Head of the Prison Camp in that area. Our immediate Camp Commander is a captain named Isobi, who spoke beautiful English and has a good reputation with a British non- coms who have been in this camp for nearly three years. We were told that no officer would be required to work. However, that work would be provided and if we would work, we would be given extra rations. At present there are two things that we can do; 1. is to assist in the building of trenches for air raid protection; 2. is to work in the garden. We have been told that we will be given an opportunity to bathe once a week. Our normal routine consists of a rising at around 5:00 AM, attending the morning roll call, immediately after which we receive either hot tea or hot water. We have about ½ hour to clean up when breakfast is served, and we go to work around 7:00 AM. At 10:00 AM we receive more hot tea or hot water and work until about 12:00 PM, where we have 1 hour off for lunch. Work again from 1:00 until 4:30 PM with the usual break at 3:00 PM for tea. Supper at 5:30 then we are free until 9:00 PM, at which time evening roll call is held in the barracks, and then all of the lights are turned off. We have been told to appoint two officers, one from the British and one from ourselves, who will report each morning to the Japanese headquarters to receive orders and to make any suggestions which might help our general welfare. We will be paid the usual 50 yen a month and have been given a small book in which to keep our accounts. If we are all only able to spend a few yen, then of course, we only report the difference between what we have spent and the 50 yen. We are to receive one Red Cross box for each two officers every two weeks or the equivalent of one box a month. As was the case in Japan, we worked 13 days and have one day off. We will be allowed to have religious services and there is a small library where reading material, in limited quantity, is available. It is by far the best set-up we have ever had.

May 5

The usual routine with only one very unfortunate incident. Colonel Beecher, in whose room I have now been placed because the Japanese felt that he was a lonely and alone, went to the Japanese headquarters and complained about the treatment of our men by the Japanese doctor, whose name I do not know. This officer, a young fanatic, is by far the hardest man we have had to deal with. Men reporting to sick call seldom are allowed to speak to him but deal entirely with the Japanese non- com or Colonel Schwartz, who has been detailed to assist the Japanese doctor. One of our men was severely handled by the Japanese doctor and Colonel Beecher, after receiving permission from the Japanese Camp Commander to see him, protested the doctor's actions. The following morning when the Japanese doctor was on duty as the Officer of the Day, and whose duty it was to check the morning roll call, came opposite to where we were standing in line, he, without provocation, beat Colonel Beecher around the head and face with both fists. When Colonel Beecher was finally knocked to the ground, the doctor proceeded to stamp on him and kick him for a minute or two. This attack was evidently warranted by the fact that Colonel Beecher had complained about the doctor's actions. Fortunately, Beecher was not too badly hurt. There is evidently nothing we can do about this outrage.

The Colonel's Way

May 23

Colonel Engelhart, who had been designated as one of the official interpreters, was caught reading a Japanese newspaper. He was slapped around a little by the Japanese soldier who caught him and then was taken to the Japanese headquarters where he was severely reprimanded and told that his case would be forwarded to the Japanese headquarters for final action. As a result, he has been confined to the barracks. He is allowed to use the bathing facilities, but outside of this he must remain in the barracks. I hope that this is all that will happen to him. The food here is quite good, but the quantity is never enough. At present, at least twice a week we are given some special food. This usually is in the form of a small fish which each officer is given, which has been fried in deep batter by the British cooks. They are very, very good. Sometimes were received french- fried onions instead of the fish but normally were given something extra in the way of food twice in every seven days. With the exception of this, we get the usual vegetable soup three times a day and a bowl of rice. As the garden yields more and more vegetables, the number in the soup increases. We have gotten potatoes for the first time since I have been a prisoner. Of course, it is so early in the season that they are quite small, but they are very filling and are very welcome. The Japanese, in their usual economic way, are not allowing our cooks to peel the potatoes, so we eat them skin and all. They are, of course, like all other vegetables, put into the soup. With the aid of the few things that we received in the Red Cross and the fact that now we have been placed on a ration which consists of rice for breakfast, a small loaf of bread about 4 ½ inches in diameter, 3 inches high, for the non -workers and some additional rice for the workers for lunch and another bowl of rice were supper, the health of the command has improved. All of the rice contains some barley which I personally like. In addition, we receive a gram a month of what we call Japanese butter. It is simply a margarine made from soya beans, and although the odor is quite strong we, of course, welcome the food as part of our regular diet. We have been issued summer uniforms, cotton two-piece uniforms, which the British tell us were captured from the Australians. Although it is quite cold, the Japanese insist that it is summer as so we put on our summer uniforms and freeze. About the only time that we are warm is when we are allowed to take a bath, which is once a week. We are excusing from work during the bath period but do not lose our work ration. One of the British officers has very kindly loaned me his short overcoat, which is a great joy. Another has given me one of his shirts and although he is about twice my size, it is very welcome as it gives me an additional shirt so that I can wash the one that the Japanese have allowed me.

June 10

Two things have happened which have been of great joy to us. First is the news of the surrender of Germany which of course has aroused a great deal of speculation as to when the main attack will be made against the Japanese mainland. I've always contested since the beginning of the war, and still hold to the premise that the Japanese will be defeated; that within six months after the surrender of Germany or before, Japan will surrender. The second factor which has added to our pleasure is the fact that the weather has now turned quite warm. Our garden is now producing quite a large quantity of vegetables which we all enjoy a great deal. The Japanese allowance for each prisoner is, however, quite small. We get around this problem by engaging the Japanese and an argument while weighing one basket, at which time another prisoner empties an un-weighed basket into the bin where the vegetables have been put. In this way we have increased our vegetable ration by at least 100%. I am still engaged in sewing on buttons and making buttonholes in cheap Japanese garments, although I have great difficulty in maintaining the quota which is required to draw a worker's ration. The problem of all of the older officers is that of glasses. Mine were lost in the sinkings and I am now using two pair of glasses which belonged to some of my less fortunate comrades.

June 27

We have lost two men recently. One of them, a fine young Captain of Ordnance. Malnutrition and army's treatment since leaving the Philippines has taken the form of edema. Colonel Schwartz tells me that it is primarily due to a lack of protein in the diet where the blood vessels are no longer able to contain the fluid which seeps into the tissues and cause is tremendous swelling. Colonel Schwartz has pleaded with the Japanese to let him use the blood plasma which he knows is in the Japanese Medical storage. His entreaties have been of no avail and he assures me that if something is not done promptly this officer will surely succumb. His predictions were certainly true, for two days after I talked to him the Captain died. He was buried in the military cemetery in Jinsen, and I must admit that the Japanese officers here gave him, insofar as they were able, with the exception of the firing squad, all of the military honors which were due to him. Our other loss, a Chief Warrant officer, who was affected with amoebic dysentery and, as in the case of the ordinance officer, the Japanese absolutely refused to give Colonel Schwartz the necessary medicine to treat him. Schwartz knew full- well that this medicine had been received through Red Cross channels and was in the Japanese Medical storage. For the older officers whose eyesight is bothering them, the Japanese have set up a new type of work. This consists of making the paper cartons which surrounds 12 boxes of ordinary safety matches, on one end of which is pasted the label of the match factory, and the other end being left open to be sealed after the matches have been placed in the carton. A great deal of argument with the Japanese has been had to establish a so-called quota of working. The Japanese claim that any Japanese school boy could make 1000 of these cartons a day. We argued that we were not Japanese school boys, and would be fortunate if we could make 100 a day. We have finally come to a settlement with the Japanese of 250 per working day. If one keeps at it, this can easily be done by about 2:30 or 3:00 PM in the afternoon. The cartons are then folded and put into bundles of 500 and evidently sold to the match manufacture. I am the senior officer in this project, and were it not for the fact that we were all so thin, making uncomfortable to sit down, it would be quite pleasant. We are able to smoke if we have any cigarettes, and of course- converse, as the work is mostly manual and certainly requires no brain effort.

July 6

Much to our surprise, the Japanese have reacted favorably to our request that some recognition be given to the 4th of July. We have teased the British a great deal about this for we were able to persuade the Japanese that this being one of our National holidays it should be given some recognition. Of course, they could not slight the British prisoners, so they enjoyed our celebration of July 4th as well as we. The Japanese asked if we wished to get off from work, which of course would have meant the loss of a day's work ration to which we replied to the negative. We were much surprised however when we were told at lunch time that we would not be required to work that afternoon and we would not lose our work ration. The Japanese gave each of us 10 pieces of candy and much to our surprise issued an extra Red Cross box two each 10 men. They also supplied us with extra rice at the noon meal, and french- fried onions and potatoes in addition to our rice and soup at the evening meal. Certainly, the war must be going against them.

July 30

Earlier in the spring the Japanese allowed the prisoners to buy about 300 tomato plants for their own use. The tomatoes which grew on these plants do not go to the Japanese kitchen at all, but are delivered directly to the barracks and divide it among us. The Japanese made a great mistake of allowing us to plant our tomatoes next to the ones in the common garden. For that reason, and the Japanese have complained bitterly, no tomatoes have ever been known to come out of the common garden, and all the ripe ones that are picked are claimed to have come from the plants which were purchased and owned exclusively by the prisoners of war. Things remain about the same. The news is a constant air and naval attack upon the Japanese mainland. Our general board of strategy feels that the attack will come sometime early in September or early October.

August 10

Something very drastic as happened as no Japanese newspapers have been published for five days. The Russians have attacked Manchuria. We all believe that the end is very near!

The Colonel's Way

Officer of the Ass't Chief of Staff; G-1
Hq. ASCOMD -APO 315
c/o PM, S.F. California, 25, June 1945

Dearest Judy:

Herewith diary #3, which has been delivered to me much sooner than I expected. It reveals, perhaps, conditions worse than those described in the two previously forwarded but Arthur's courage never wavered, and I <u>know</u> that it will carry him through. You may be disturbed by the thought that many people have read these. You must realize, however the every word in it is of the utmost importance to the War and State Departments, and that each name - both Japanese and American - must be carefully documented and annotated by the Section in charge of that work in Manila. Had I not appeared on the scene, you would have received the diaries [the originals] and still will, through the Adjunct Generals' Department, but not for months. Over two hundred diaries were recovered and are being transcribed alphabetically. As the work has just begun, I went to work on a friend of mine and was able to get Arthur's diaries done immediately. I must caution you, unnecessarily I am sure, that no publicity concerning the diaries - not even the fact of their existence - much must be allowed. Remember Arthur is still a prisoner. For your information, the diaries were recovered at Cabanatuan, having been buried in a predetermined spot, wrapped in newspapers and rags and encased in old tin cans. My love to you and the boys-

Devotedly,/s/ Bill

EPILOGUE

On September 7, 1945 Arthur was back in the U. S. Army's hands and evacuated by the U.S. Seventh Division on September 23rd. His brother, Bill, was right on top of it all and sent several wires from Headquarters in China, anxious to hear from him right away. Of the original 12,000 American POWs, less than 250 American POWs, [according to my grandfather's sworn testimony] boarded a ship bound for San Francisco, and he was among them.

As soon as he could, he sent flowers to Judy with a simple note: *"From the boy whose only joy is loving you"*; [a line from Bing Crosby's song: 'Remember Me']. She knew then, he was okay. In San Francisco, he was briefly admitted to Letterman General Hospital. He called home and he and my grandmother decided to cut the travel time in half and both caught a train to Chicago and reunited at the Palmer House Hotel. It must have been a grand moment! When they got back to the east coast, Arthur was considered to be in only 'fair' shape and was admitted to Woodrow Wilson General Hospital in Staunton, VA where he remained until February 1946. In the following months, he signed papers swearing him to secrecy on the *"...unannounced organizations which have assisted evaders and escapers, identifying the helpers of evaders ...and equipment for evasion and escape and other special activities within prison camps which constitute intelligence information."* I estimate that my grandfather smuggled in around $2500.00, maybe more, of his own money from the Patapsco State Bank in Maryland, which is around $34,000.00 in 2015 currency.

And, recommendation letters to honor his remarkable service began to pour in. Up until now, he had earned his Aviator Wings and The WWI Victory Medal with Bronze Star. General George Parker recommended Arthur for the Distinguished Service Medal for the time under his command; [Nov. 1941- Feb. 1942] , but was not favorably considered. Instead, General Funk, General Jones and Colonel Dennis Moore wrote letters recommending the Legion of Merit award. The Colonel received an award for almost every phase of the Philippine Campaign; from the day after Pearl Harbor until surrender, to his service as G-4 on General King's staff to his, *"... exceptionally outstanding service and meritorious performance of duties as Group and Camp Executive Officer at Cabanatuan...with his zealous, energetic, unselfish and persistent actions he greatly aided in regaining and maintaining discipline, improving morale, bettering sanitary conditions and exacting an honest distribution of food and supplies. He demonstrated outstanding leadership under the most difficult circumstances which resulted in improving the living conditions of thousands of American Prisoners of War."*

One of his Bronze Stars Medals was awarded for his humanitarianism during and after The Death March and is particularly touching as it recalls the time in the diaries where Arthur asks General King if he can take charge of the water situation at Camp O'Donnell. With only one spigot for water, my grandfather not only organizes the water for the 10,000 American POWs streaming in from the Death March but the Filipino Army as well- **100,000 men**! It reads: *"For meritorious achievement while a Prisoner of War of the Japanese for volunteering to perform the arduous tasks of securing and distributing food and water, conducting to shelter and caring for the columns of prisoners as they reached Camp O'Donnell during the period 10-28th April, 1942. These duties were performed for the good of the prisoners as a whole under extremely difficult conditions and while this officer was suffering from malnutrition."*

The Colonel [second in line] receiving his Legion of Merit award and one of his Bronze Stars w/ Oak Leaf cluster from 3 star General Albert Wedemeyer; Oct. 23, 1946

The Colonel's Way

His list of awards for The Philippine Campaign and Civil Service are as follows:

~The Legion of Merit
~The Bronze Star with Oak Leaf Cluster
~ The Purple Heart
~ The American Defense Medal with Bronze Star
~ The National Defense Service Medal
~ The Philippine Defense Medal with two Bronze Stars
~ The Philippine Liberation Medal
~ The Asiatic/Pacific Theatre Medal with two Bronze Stars
~ The Foreign Service clasp
~ The WWII Victory Medal
~ The Presidential Unit Citation with two Oak Leaf Clusters
~ The Philippine Presidential Unit Citation
~The Army Commendation Ribbon
~ 7 O' Seas Bars
~ The POW Medal [(posthumously]

Lt. Col. Johnny Johnson went on to be our second youngest Army Chief of Staff ever, serving during the Vietnam years, and became a four-star general. But, he will never be forgotten for the staggering $750,000.00 worth of goods and food [over $10 million in 2015 currency] he smuggled into Cabanatuan. [Interestingly enough, even after "High Pockets" is arrested, you'll notice that my grandfather's checks from Maryland keep coming, as does food and supplies into the Commissary, which raises more questions than it answers.]

Carl Engelhart survived as well and retired in 1950. He received many medals including the POW Medal, the Bronze Star and the Purple Heart. He went back to his national pistol shooting competitions [winning over 100 medals and awards] as well as serving the community. Col. David S. Babcock, Arthur's close companion, also received one of the five Legion of Merit awards given during this time and I am sure many other decorations.

    As my grandfather and grandmother settled into 'Our Decision' in Howard County, which was now a year-round residence, he discovers that he was busted back to Lt. Colonel for being 'beleaguered' and 'missing in action' as a POW. He lost the letter from General King of his field promotion in April of '42 to full-bird colonel in the sinking of the Oryoku Maru and has no real record to prove his rank. Luckily, in a long and drawn out process, General King and others provide what they can in letters reconstructing that time of chaos before the fall of Bataan. In correspondences that would last well into 1947, Arthur fights to get his rank of colonel reinstated and the $1590.02 he is due in back pay. He does get his rank and his pay… but then, in another twist, the Comptroller of Finance for the Army states it was a "disallowed" voucher and the United States wants their money **back!** In a push n' pull case that stretches into 1951, Arthur continues to protest on his own behalf- but he can't fully because he's been sworn to secrecy on what happened in Cabanatuan and the thousands of dollars he personally smuggled in for his men from his own bank account! So he enlists help from the senior Maryland Senator, J. Millard Tawes, and Representative George H. Fallon who take his case all the way to Washington! Representative Fallon introduces Bill #4353 into Congress for the "release of liability" of the Colonel to refund the money- and it passes June 6, 1951.

    In the meantime, he has assumed the position of District Executive of the Maryland Military District and Senior Army Advisor to the Army Reserve /National Guard in Maryland. Arthur would testify at the War Crimes Office, January 16, 1948 [in the

presence of Jack S. Kelly, Special Agent, 109th CIC Det., Second Army] against the Japanese as they clearly violated the rules of war, [Geneva Convention]. In 1950, he was named Chief of the Maryland Military District where he remained until he retired from military life on December 31, 1952.

My grandfather was always a grateful man but he had his limits. He was bitter over his battle to regain his rank and the fact that in order to be promoted to Brigadier General he would have to up-root his family and move to Panama. My grandmother, and even my grandfather, [according to the retirement letter] expresses concern and claims "personal hardship" as a reason to retire a year before he is able. He and others, like Mayor of Baltimore D'Alesandro, petition for his 'early' retirement in 1952, instead of 1953. Part of the reason is that Judy's mother has to move into Our Decision and she is quite ill. He also has two sons in college at the time and he loves his farm and doesn't want to leave *again*.

Before he retires from the Military District, he is asked to present his troops from the National Guard and Reserves at the opening ceremonies for the Chesapeake Bay Bridge in July 1952. Again, in stellar style, he adds color and panache to the ceremonies and gets a letter thanking him from the State of Maryland. In the meantime, another cruel twist; even though he's gotten his rank back and released from the pay refund, he has to petition to get this put into permanent record with the Army Records Board as the Department of the Army disagrees with all of what has transpired around this case. Arthur hires a lawyer from Washington in May of 1953, a Eugene Carusi, who appears with him at the hearing at the Pentagon December 16, 1953 as my grandfather testifies to the long journey he has been on to rectify the question of his field promotion. Finally, after the hearing, it's settled and in fact-suggests to them a law be enacted after this case so that it doesn't happen again.

Arthur goes onto being appointed Deputy Director of the Maryland Civil Defense Agency by Governor Theodore McKeldin in 1953. He resigns this post to become the manager of The Maryland Operational Survival Project which was a project of the Federal government to devise a plan in the event of nuclear attack. The project ended in June, 1959 so Arthur was appointed Director of the Baltimore City Civil Defense Agency by then Governor J. Millard Tawes where he remained until full retirement in December, 1961.

My grandfather was a member of The Society of Cincinnati, The Howard County Hunt Club, The Elkridge Country

The Colonel's Way

Club and The Bachelors Cotillion. Because of the latter, in the late 1940s and into 1950, Sandy and his brother were on the circuit of what was to be the last 'grand age' of socializing and cotillions. My father owned a white tie and tails, and black tie and tails and used them frequently as he gained a reputation as one of the handsomest and nicest young men around. He was even nicknamed 'Adonis' at one point, and is fondly remembered even today by the ladies as 'divine'. His best friend, Charlie Carroll, was among the Maryland elite; a descendant of the Carrolls of Carrollton, and lived at Doughoregan Manor [originally 13,500 acres] near Ellicott City. My father would visit him there and I am sure, went to parties there as well. The house was 300 feet long and had a full-sized chapel built on one end. The manor is still occupied today by the Carroll family and still maintains over 900 acres. On October 25, 1950 my father enlisted with The Maryland National Guard. He graduated from Artillery School and the Battery Officers Course in 1952 as a 2nd lieutenant. He left the Guard in 1958 as a captain.

Sadly, on February 2nd 1961; in what will go down as one of the coldest days on record in Maryland [- 5 degrees], my grandfather was down in the basement with a blow-torch thawing out the kitchen pipes at Our Decision. He thawed the pipes, but was unaware that the galvanized pipe elbows must have sparked the insulation behind the wall and before they knew it, their house [circa early 1800s], was an inferno of old, dry wood. The Ellicott City Fire Department rushed out with 500 gallons of water, but once that was gone, there was no liquid water anywhere. They even broke the ice on the pool but it cracked the concrete and the remaining water drained out. They watched it burn to the ground until all that remained was the five chimneys, the silver they managed to salvage, some furniture and *each other*. Luckily, they were able to rebuild Our Decision, but I was told it was never the same.

Somewhere in the late 1960s, his stint in the Philippines finally reared its ugly head. At Woodrow Wilson Hospital, his medical report stated that they *did* find trace amounts of microscopic hematuria and ova of schistosoma in his urine. In fact, he had picked up Schistosomiasis, a disease caused by a parasite that burrows through the skin. It showed up as complications in his kidneys, eventually developing into kidney cancer. He was operated on in early 1969 and died just three weeks later at Fort George Meade in Anne Arundel County. Chef Robert, now in his mid-nineties, was there to see him receive full military honors at his burial at St. John's Episcopal Church [circa 1728] which flew the flag at half- mast for the first time since the Civil War. Buried on top of a hill under a tree, he isn't far from Our Decision.

We'll never know all the details, but it was Judy and Arthur's decision to stay together until the end, despite what had happened while he was away. I imagine he wanted to remember all the living he did and not the dying he saw. His dear Judy had done her duties on the home front and essentially 'made decisions based on the landscape of the moment.'

I think we can all say with some conviction that we are grateful Arthur joined the Army instead of staying in banking or surveying! Decorations aside, how do you ever thank a man like Arthur for his amazing and relentless service? He will always be remembered as a kind man of deep emotion with a rare combination of charisma and leadership qualities who did things for others knowing he'd never be repaid. May we all learn something from the Colonel; a man whose love was always stronger.

EXTRA PHOTOS

Baby Arthur & mother; 1898   Arthur as a young boy.

Arthur in his youth.   Arthur and Bill in the 1930s at Ocean City, MD.

L. G. 'Bill' Shreve

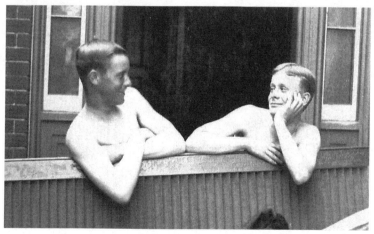

Arthur's father, [Arthur L.,Sr. on the left] looking at his brother, Oswald Tilghman Shreve, 1888 in Baltimore.

Above: Arthur, Judy, Bill and Barbara Shreve and guest at The 2 O'Clock Club in Baltimore City.

Arthur and Prince Gerald on the left and "You'll Do II" on the right. Prince Gerald is the heavy weight hunter that Arthur will bring east with him when he comes.

The Colonel's Way

Below: Sketch of a "Hell Ship"

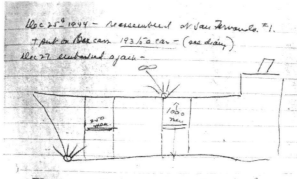

The Colonel's Way

Above; Arthur - 1917 at the School of Aeronautics, Un. of Illinois

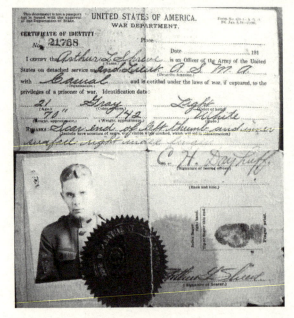

HEADQUARTERS TWENTY FIRST INFANTRY BRIGADE,
OFFICE OF THE BRIGADE COMMANDER

Schofield Barracks, H. T.

Oct-27- 1922

My dear Mr. Shreve:

The discharge of Lieut. Will leaves me without a personal aide. How would you like the job? Be perfectly frank about it. If it does not appeal to you or if you think it will in any way hurt your career do not hesitate to say so. Whatever your decision it will be respected.

In case you are agreeably disposed to proposition I will make application for your detail.

Very sincerely

Joseph E. ___
Brig. Gen. ___

Lt. Arthur J. Shreve
8th F.A.

82D CONGRESS
1ST SESSION
H. R. 4353

IN THE HOUSE OF REPRESENTATIVES

JUNE 6, 1951

Mr. FALLON introduced the following bill; which was referred to the Committee on the Judiciary

A BILL

For the relief of Colonel Arthur L. Shreve.

1 *Be it enacted by the Senate and House of Representa-*
2 *tives of the United States of America in Congress assembled,*
3 That all liability to the United States arising out of the
4 payment to Arthur L. Shreve, O-11176, colonel, United
5 States Army, of the sum of $1,590.02, representing the
6 difference between the pay and allowances of the grade of
7 colonel and the pay and allowances of the grade of lieutenant
8 colonel for the period from April 7, 1942, through Septem-

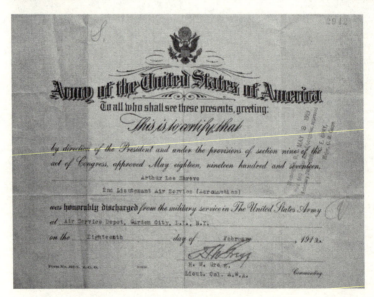

Early photos of Arthur/ by Arthur - horses & caissons

The Colonel's Way

TERMS & ABBREVIATIONS

AA- Anti aircraft
BRIG- Brigadier
BTN- Battalion
BTY- Battery
CAC- Combined Arms Command
CAG – Carrier Air Group
Camote- native sweet potato
Carametta- bull cart
Carabao - cow
Cassava- native melon
CHAP- Chaplain
CO- Commanding Officer
COL- Colonel
CP- Command Post
DET- Detail
EM- Enlisted man
FA- Field Artillery
FO- Field Officer
Ganta – [also gantangan] –measure /volume, almost a kilogram
GEN- General
LT- Lieutenant
Lugao- rice gruel
Nisei- Japanese immigrants, born & educated in the USA
P- peso
Panutsa- sugar cake
MG- Machine gun
PA- Philippine Army
POW- Prisoner of War
PVT- Private
SGT- Sergeant
USA- United States Army
USN- United States Navy
USMC- United States Marine Corps

The Colonel's Way

REFERENCES & NOTES

"*Be Thou At Peace & Memorial Articles.*" West Point Association of Graduates. N.p., n.d. Web. 29 Sept. 2014.
<http://www.westpointaog.org/memorials>.

Diary of Lt. Col. Arthur L. Shreve, Jr. (F.A.) G.S.C., Diaries and Historical Narratives, Entry A1 1067, Records of the Adjutant General's Office, Record Group 407, Box 143, The National Archives at College Park, College Park, Maryland.

Intelligence Activities in the Philippines during the Japanese Occupation. N.p.: General Headquarters, United States Army Forces, Pacific, 1948. paperlessarchives.com, n.d. Web.
<http://www.paperlessarchives.com/FreeTitles/PhilippinesInteliigenceActivitie.pdf>.

"*Keijo and Jinsen POW Camps in Korea.*" Keijo and Jinsen POW Camps in Korea. N.p., n.d. Web. 27 Oct. 2014.
<http://www.mansell.com/pow_resources/camplists/other/korea-main.html>.

"*Perpetuation of Testimony of Arthur L. Shreve.*" Perpetuation of Testimony of Arthur L. Shreve. Mansell.com, n.d. Web. 20 Oct. 2014.
<http://www.mansell.com/pow_resources/camplists/fukuoka/fuk_01_fukuoka/fukuoka_01/Shreve.html>.

1. Col. Eugene C. Jacobs, *Blood Brothers; A Medics Sketchbook,* [Carlton Press, New York - 1985] p.64-67
2. "   "   ", p. 59, 64

The Colonel's Way

ABOUT THE AUTHOR
Heather Perrine Shreve
{artist, writer, speaker}

Heather was born in Baltimore County, Maryland in 1963 and was raised on a small farm where she became attracted to the natural beauty of her surroundings. The rustic landscapes (and the creatures in them) were her first subjects captured on paper; both in art and writings. She began selling her art around age eleven and from there it became a passion and a vocation.

In 1983 at age 19, Heather went to Africa on a zoological expedition across Kenya. There, she discovered a land of massive size and rustic beauty that resonated with her on a level that has never been surpassed. As she crossed the beautiful country, she unwittingly got caught up in the black market ivory trade when she mistakenly bought an ivory bracelet from the Maasai. Later, in Mombasa, Heather was arrested and jailed in a harrowing experience that she would later recount in writing and use as a leadership keynote speech.

After being married and having two children, Heather became divorced in 2008 and rediscovered her love of writing once again. Now, Heather has put her efforts into writing screenplays and other stories based in history, real characters and life events. As she continues to write, Heather will always be compelled to paint as she now has logged over 30,000 hours behind the brush.

Since becoming an ACSM certified Well Coach and personal trainer in 2010, Heather has written six books including two health workbooks, and several non-fiction books: *Caught on the Equator*; [two versions], *The Art of Becoming* and *The Colonel's Way*. History has always been an interest, but now- with her grandfather's story under her belt- she has taken her speaking career to a new level. Her goal is to demonstrate greatness and the power of action throughout American history with stellar stories of other fearless leaders who have contributed so much to our nation's progress.

You can find Heather's books, including *The Colonel's Way* both on her web site: http://www.heather-shreve.com and Amazon. Please contact her there to book a future speaking engagement at your next event or conference.

The Colonel's Way

Made in the USA
Middletown, DE
09 August 2015